Ray Yarmac

SELF CONCEPT
AND
SCHOOL
ACHIEVEMENT

SELF CONCEPT
AND
SCHOOL
ACHIEVEMENT

William Watson Purkey
University of Florida

PRENTICE-HALL, INC., Englewood Cliffs, New Jersey

Current printing (last digit):
10   9   8

Printed in the United States of America

Prentice-Hall International, Inc., London
Prentice-Hall of Australia, Pty. Ltd., Sydney
Prentice-Hall of Canada, Ltd., Toronto
Prentice-Hall of India Private Limited, New Delhi
Prentice-Hall of Japan, Inc., Tokyo

PREFACE

A fresh, exciting, and humanistic development in contemporary education is the growing emphasis placed on the student's subjective and personal evaluation of himself, a dominant influence on his success in school. This development is fresh because the self concept has been virtually ignored by psychology and largely overlooked by education. It is exciting because it provides teachers with a set of unifying principles which ties together seemingly unrelated aspects of life in classrooms and allows them to understand and influence the conduct of students. It is humanistic because it cares about the individual and is primarily concerned with what takes place in his personal world.

In Chapter 1 of this little book an overview of theories about the self is presented, which provides a brief history and some important characteristics of the self. In Chapter 2 we explore the strong and persistent relationship between the self concept and academic achievement, and show why there is deepening discontent with the notion that human ability is the overwhelming factor in academic success. In Chapter 3 we explain how the self begins, how it develops in social interaction, and what happens to it under the impact of school. Finally, in Chapter 4, we suggest ways for the teacher to become a significant force in building positive and realistic self concepts in students.

"Self theory" is neither an established fact nor an all-inclusive theory of human existence. Some students who esteem themselves highly do not show commensurate achievement in school, (Brookover, 1967), and some researchers (Schwarz, 1967, Peters, 1968) have not found an inevitable relationship between self-esteem and scholastic success. However, the overwhelming body of contemporary research points insistently to the relationship

v

between self-esteem and academic achievement and suggests strongly that the self concept can no longer be ignored by parents and teachers. The purpose of this book is to help make what we know about the self concept an important part of what goes on in schools.

A grateful acknowledgment is made to all those who helped me in the preparation of this book. Especially deep is my indebtedness to three significant people in my life: my colleague, Dr. Arthur W. Combs, who taught me about perceptual psychology, my graduate assistant, Mr. Jim Bowers, who helped me in so many ways; and above all, my wife Imogene, whose love and encouragement was, and is, indispensable.

William Watson Purkey, Sr.
Gainesville, Florida

CONTENTS

Acknowledgements

"Birches" from *Complete Poems of Robert Frost*. Copyright 1916 by Holt, Rine-hart and Winston, Inc. Copyright 1944 by Robert Frost. By permission of Holt, Rinehart and Winston, Inc., and John Cape Ltd.

To Kill a Mockingbird by Harper Lee. Copyright 1960 by Harper Lee. By per-mission of J.B. Lippincott Company.

The Razor's Edge by W. Somerset Maugham. By permission of the Literary Executor of W. Somerset Maugham, William Heineman Ltd., and Doubleday and Company, Inc., Publishers.

Joseph in Egypt by Thomas Mann. By permission of Alfred A. Knopf, Inc., and Martin Secker & Warburg Ltd.

Ovid's *Metamorphoses* (Everyman's Library Edition). By permission of E.P. Dutton & Co. Inc. and J.M. Dent & Sons Ltd.: Publishers.

Peanuts by Charles Schultz. Copyright 1966 by United Feature Syndicate. By permission.

chapter one

INTRODUCTION TO THEORIES OF THE SELF

*Oh, wad some power the giftie gie us
To see oursels as ithers see us!
It wad frae monie a blunder
    free us,
      An' foolish notion. . . .*

Robert Burns, *To A Louse*

It was "one evening deep in June . . . mid-summer, to be exact," when the story begins of "The Mouse and Henry Carson." In this fable of the influence of attitudes on academic achievement, Lowry (1961) describes how a mouse ran into the office of the Educational Testing Service and accidentally triggered a delicate point in the apparatus just as the College Entrance Examination Board's data on one Henry Carson was being scored.

Henry was an average high-school student who was unsure of himself and his abilities. Had it not been for the mouse, Henry's scores would have been average or less, but the mouse changed all that, for the scores which emerged from the computer were amazing—800's in both the verbal and quantitative areas.

When the scores reached Henry's school, the word of his giftedness spread like wildfire. Teachers began to reevaluate their gross underestimation of this fine lad, counselors trembled at the thought of neglecting such talent, and even college admissions officers began to recruit Henry for their schools.

New worlds opened for Henry, and as they opened he started to grow as a person and as a student. Once he became aware of his potentialities and began to be treated differently by the significant people in his life, a form of self-fulfilling prophecy took place. Henry gained in confidence and began "to put his mind in the way of great things." Lowry ends the story of "The Mouse and Henry Carson" by saying that Henry became one of the best men of his generation.

The story illustrates two major propositions of this book—that the ways in which a student views himself and his world are (1) products of how others see him; and (2) primary forces in his academic achievement. This emphasis on the individual's perceptions is different from the older and better-known positions of psychoanalysis (emphasizing unconscious motivations) and behaviorism (emphasizing actual behavior), in that it stresses personal awareness (perception) as an active agent in determining conduct. It suggests that if teachers are to understand the behavior of the people with whom they work, then it is necessary to learn to see things from their point of view. This general approach is sometimes called "perceptual psychology" because it gives primary importance to a person's perceived world, rather than to objective reality.

Gradually, it is becoming clear that many of the difficulties which people experience in most areas of life are closely connected with the ways they see themselves and the world in which they live. The evidence presented in this book indicates that students' failures in basic subjects, as well as the misdirected motivation and lack of commitment characteristic of the underachiever, the dropout, and the socially disabled, are in large measure the consequence of faulty perceptions of themselves and the world.

In Chapter 2 we review studies whose import seems to be that students' difficulties in basic academic skills are directly related to their *beliefs* that they cannot read, write, handle numbers, or think accurately, rather than to basic differences in *capacity*. In other words, many students have difficulty in school not because of low intelligence, poor eyesight, poverty, or whatever, but because they have learned to see themselves as incapable of handling academic work or to see the work as irrelevant to their perceptual worlds. There is reason to believe that these factors may also operate to restrict participation in special school activities such as athletics, dramatics, public speaking, student government, music, and clubs.

More and more there is a deepening interest in the individual's perception of himself and his situation as a major influence on his behavior. Recent books by Hamachek (1965), Diggory (1966), Coopersmith (1967), Rosenthal and Jacobson (1968b), Gale (1969), and others illustrate this interest. To understand this wellspring of interest in theories about the self, it helps to take a quick look at its development.

BRIEF HISTORY OF THEORIES OF THE SELF

It is probable that our more reflective ancestors, huddled around a fire in some forgotten cave, pulled their animal skins close around their shoulders and passed the time thinking about their fears, their desires, and how they felt about themselves. Some time during this dawn of man's history man began to give serious thought to his nonphysical, psychological self. Later, with the advent of written history, writers would describe this awareness of self in terms of spirit, psyche or soul. During the Middle Ages the concept of soul was further developed by theologians, who stressed its immortality and superiority to the body in which it dwelled.

A turning point in man's thinking about his non-physical being came in 1644, when René Descartes wrote his *Principles of Philosophy*. Descartes proposed that doubt was a principal tool of disciplined inquiry, yet he could not doubt that he doubted. He reasoned that if he doubted, he was thinking, and therefore he must exist. Other philosophers of this period, among them Spinoza and Leibnitz, added their ideas about the mystery of the nonphysical aspect of man. Terms such as mind, soul, psyche, and self were often used interchangeably, with scant regard for an invariant vocabulary or scientific experimentation. For the most part, a general state of confusion in regard to the concept of self existed into the present century.

A milestone in the quest for understanding internal processes was the voluminous writing of Sigmund Freud (1900, 1911, 1923, 1933, 1938). Freud gave attention to the self under the concept of ego development and functioning. This concept of ego was given increased attention by his daughter Anna (1946), who built a respected place for it in therapy. Yet, as Munroe (1955) suggests, the Freudians and neo-Freudians generally hesitated to make the self a primary psychological unit or to give it central importance in their theoretical formulations.

At the turn of the present century, when American psychology began to take its place among the other academic disciplines, there was a great deal of interest in the self. For example, when William James wrote his *Principles of Psychology* (1890), his chapter on "The Consciousness of Self" was the longest in the two volumes. Yet during this period, American psychology was on the verge of a revolution.

Thanks to a hectic period of theory building, followed by strongly held positions on issues, most psychologists rallied around certain systems and organized schools which were characterized by ardent advocacy of their own theory and unrestrained hostility to opposing ones. Freudian psychologists emphasized unconscious motivation, introspectionists defended the process of introspection as a way of exploring consciousness, gestaltists believed in the value of insight and stressed the selective perceiver, and the behaviorists attempted, with surprising success, to cancel out all other schools by claiming that all systems except their own studied consciousness while only a person's tangible, observable behavior was fit for scientific inquiry.

When the smoke cleared, the behaviorism of J. B. Watson (1925) had carried the day. Psychology was redirected, attention was turned to observable stimuli and response, and the inner life of the individual was labeled as beyond the scope of psychology. The self as a psychological construct was pushed into limbo, along with such internal constructs as mind, consciousness, and awareness. As Wylie (1961) points out, during the 1920's through the 1940's, the self received scant attention from the behavior-oriented psychologists who dominated American psychology.

An interesting sidelight to all this is that psychological theories have always had a strong influence on education. Through the years teachers have followed the prescriptions of psychologists, from William James with his emphasis on self, to Sigmund Freud with his focus on unconscious motivations, to J. B. Watson with his stress on observable and measurable behavior. So it happened that when psychology abandoned the self, so did education.

Although the decline of interest in the self was encouraged and cheered by behavioristic psychologists, all the fault for its neglect cannot be laid at their door. As Diggory (1966) explains in his comprehensive review of theories about the self, very little of the literature on the self during those early years described experiments or contained references to experimental psychology. Those few who advocated the importance of the self weakened their position by their neglect of rigorous experimentation.

Whatever the cause, emphasis on the self declined as a concern of American psychology and education during the first half of this century. However, there were a few exceptions to this general neglect. George H. Mead (1934) made the concept of self a major part of his theoretical writing on the philosophy of society and described in detail how the self is developed through transactions with the environment. He argued that personality, rather than being anchored on biological variables, was determined by social-psychological factors. Lewin (1935) viewed the self as a central and relatively permanent organization which gave consistency to the entire personality. Goldstein (1939) analyzed the processes of self-actualization, as contrasted with those of the sick organism which must constantly worry about bodily preservation. This was a forerunner of the comprehensive work of Maslow (1954, 1956) who has written so powerfully on self-actualization. Prescott Lecky (1945) contributed the notion of self-consistency as a primary motivating force in human behavior. Bertocci (1945) emphasized the two aspects of the self, distinguishing between the self as object, "me," and the self as subject, "I". Murphy (1947) discussed the origins and modes of self-enhancement and how the self is related to the social group. Raimy (1948) introduced measures of self concept in counseling interviews and argued that psychotherapy is a process of changing the self concept. Hilgard, in his presidential address before the American Psychological Association (1949) defended the thesis that all defense mechanisms imply a self-reference, and that the self can be a unifying concept in problems of motivation. Gordon Allport (1937, 1943, 1955, 1961) throughout his career emphasized the importance of self in contemporary psychology and argued for a purposeful, rational man, aware of himself and controlling his future through his aspirations. As Diggory notes "The fact that the new self psychologists (e.g., Allport) were able to argue substantive matters of learning theory and motivation with the heirs of the behaviorists made the latter pay attention, and finally to agree that there might be something to the idea of self after all" (1966, p. 57).

Among the most consistent in objecting to behaviorism were the clinical psychologists who found the tenets of behaviorism too narrow and passive to account for most human behavior. One of the most eloquent and significant voices was that of Carl Rogers. In a series of articles, books, and lectures, Carl Rogers (1947; 1951; 1954; 1959a, b; 1965; 1969) presented a system of psychotherapy called "nondirective," which was built around the importance of the self in human adjustment. In Rogers' theory, the self is *the* central aspect of personality. He viewed the self as a phenomenological concept (a pattern of conscious perceptions experienced by the individual) which is of central importance to that individual's behavior and adjustment. Rogers described the self as a social product, developing out of interpersonal relationships and striving for consistency. He believed that there is a need for positive regard both from others and from oneself, and that in every human being there is a tendency toward self-actualization and growth so long as this is permitted by the environment. Rogers' system went far towards linking together earlier notions about the self. In fact, his impact was so great that his general approach soon became known as "self theory." An excellent review of Rogers' basic assumptions is presented by Patterson (1961).

Another notable influence in reintroducing the concept of the self into psychology and education was the writing of Combs and Snygg. In their 1949 book *Individual Behavior* (2nd ed., 1959) they proposed that the basic drive of the individual is the maintenance and enhancement of the self. They further declared that all behavior, without exception, is dependent upon the individual's personal frame of reference. In other words, behavior is determined by the totality of experience of which an individual is aware of at an instant of action, his "phenomenal field." Combs and Snygg's insistence on giving major importance to the ways in which people see themselves and their worlds was a significant contribution to psychology and education.

In the last few years there has been an enthusiastic rebirth of interest in internal and intrinsic motivating forces and cognitive and symbolic processes, particularly with reference to the dynamic importance of the self. The research and writing of Brookover (1959, 1962, 1964, 1965, 1967), Heider (1958), Patterson (1959, 1961), Combs (1965, 1969), Diggory (1966), and Cooper-smith (1967), among others, have given us a deeper understanding of the dynamics of the self in determining behavior. Taking as our vantage point this rich and newly plowed field of writing and research, we will look at some major characteristics of the self.

CHARACTERISTICS OF THE SELF

> *The world has many centers, one for each created being,*
> *And about each one lieth in its own circle.*
> *Thou standeth but half an ell from me,*
> *Yet about thee lieth a universe whose center I am not,*
> *But thou art.*
>
> Thomas Mann, *Joseph in Egypt*

From various definitions of the self given by Lecky (1945), Rogers (1951), Jersild (1952), and Combs and Snygg (1959), we can arrive at a composite definition of the "self" as *a complex and dynamic system of beliefs which an individual holds true about himself, each belief with a corresponding value.* This definition highlights two important characteristics of the self: it is *organized*, and it is *dynamic*. These characteristics may be illustrated by a drawing.

The weakness in using a drawing to represent the self lies in our tendency to oversimplify a many-faceted and multiple-layered constellation of ideas. Yet analogies do help us to understand, and it may be helpful for the reader to refer to the drawing from time to time as we explore the organized and dynamic qualities of the self.

The Self is Organized

There is agreement among researchers that the self has a generally stable quality which is characterized by harmony and orderliness. Please look at the drawing and imagine the large spiral as representing this unity of organization of the self. This whole is made up of subparts which are shown as small spirals, each of which may be fairly well organized but which is a part of the

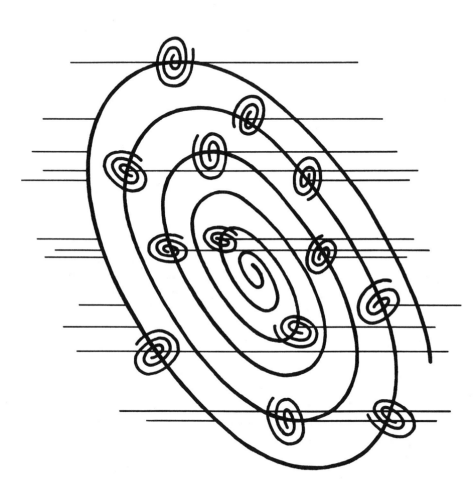

total self. These smaller spirals represent beliefs which one holds about oneself. These beliefs may be divided into categories (student, Negro, husband, American, tennis player, Christian) and attributes (strong, tall, ugly, young, friendly). A person has countless beliefs about himself, not all equally significant. Some beliefs are very close to the essence of the self, and so these are pictured as closer to the center of the large spiral. Others, less central and important, are pictured toward the outside of the self. Lowe (1961) has reasoned that some parts of the self concept are peripheral to the core of the self and are therefore unstable, while other parts are central to the self and are therefore highly resistant to change. Anyone who has given up a lightly held belief about himself, or fought for a cherished one, can visualize this process. In her analytic study of individuals in distress, Horney (1939) found that most persons cling to their pretensions "as a drowning man grasps at a straw." Closely held beliefs about oneself are difficult to change.

A second organizational feature of the self is that each concept (smaller spiral) in the system has its own generally negative or positive value. This dimension, value, is illustrated in the drawing by the horizontal lines. Each of the smaller concepts in the large self has value. For example, being an Indian might be very close to the center of the self but could be valued negatively by the experiencing individual. He might think: "I am aware most of the time of being an Indian. Being an Indian is a central part of me. But it's not good to be an Indian."

A third organized quality of the self is how success and failure are generalized throughout the system. Diggory (1966) discovered from his research that when one ability is important and highly rated, a failure of that ability lowers one's self-evaluation of other, seemingly unrelated, abilities. Conversely, the success of an important and highly rated ability raises the self-evaluation of other abilities. A similar finding of such spread of effect is reported by Ludwig and Maehr (1967). Returning to our drawing on page 8, imagine each concept (small spiral) to be a tiny bell. When one is rung, all the others chime in, echoing the original bell. For instance, if you think you're a good cook and cooking is highly valued by you, repeated failure in the kitchen will lower your self-esteem in other seemingly unrelated areas.

A final organizational quality of the self is that it is wonderfully unique. Like fingerprints, no two people ever hold identical sets of beliefs about themselves. This uniqueness of the self, which makes for an infinite variety of personalities, helps to explain problems of communication. Since no two people ever see themselves or the world in the same way, it is difficult for them to agree about what they experience. A middle-aged, middle-class, white, female schoolteacher must work hard to understand the perceptual world of a black youngster from the ghetto.

The Self is Dynamic

Perhaps the single most important assumption of modern theories about the self is that the maintenance and enhancement of the perceived self is the motive behind all behavior (Snygg and Combs, 1949; Rogers, 1951; Combs and Snygg, 1959). In other words, each of us is constantly striving to maintain, protect, and enhance the self of which he is aware. If this is true, then it follows that experience is perceived in terms of its relevance to the self and that behavior is determined by these perceptions. Let's examine these ideas more closely.

The self as a vantage point As Combs and Snygg commented: "The self is the individual's basic frame of reference, the central core, around which the remainder of the perceptual field is organized. In this sense, the phenomenal self is both product of the individual's experience and producer of whatever new experience he is capable of" (1959, p. 146). This means that everything is comprehended from the personal self-referent vantage point; the world exists for the individual only as he is conscious of it. Rollo May expressed it this way: "We cannot . . . stand outside our own skin and perch on some Archimedes point, and have a way of surveying experience that does not itself depend upon the assumptions that one makes about the nature of man, or the nature of whatever one is studying" (1961, p. 290). Things are significant or insignificant, important or unimportant, attractive or unattractive, valuable or worthless, in terms of their relationship to oneself. We evaluate the world and its meaning in terms of how we see ourselves. Many students do poorly in school simply because what the school is doing seems irrelevant to himself and his world.

As general assumptions, we can say that if a potentially new concept of himself appears to the individual to be *consistent with and relevant to* the concepts already present in his systematized view of himself, it is accepted and assimilated easily. If the concept appears to have *no relation or relevance* to that system, it is generally ignored. And if it is *inconsistent and uncongenial* with the system, it is likely to be rejected or distorted. In practical terms, these assumptions mean that an "A" student will accept fresh classroom victories easily, while success is tough to handle for the student who has met many failures. A student who considers himself a failure at school will reject or distort evidence which contradicts his perceived self, no matter how flattering the information may be or how helpful it may appear from another person's point of view. As Jersild suggests, the child is active "in the maintenance of the self picture, even if by misfortune the picture is a false and unhealthy one" (1952, p. 14).

Several studies (Aronson and Mills, 1959; Aronson and Carlsmith, 1962) have shown that students who did poorly but expected to do so were more satisfied and contented than even those who did well but had not expected to do so. Those who found themselves doing well experienced considerable discomfort and tended to bring their performance into agreement with their expectations. Individuals are generally unwilling to accept evidence that is contrary to the ways they perceive themselves; they resolve conflict between evidence and personal judgment in favor of personal judgment. For example, if you see yourself as a good teacher and being a good teacher is a central aspect of yourself and of great value, it will take a large number of classroom failures to convince you to think otherwise.

There are times when the self-image appears to shift abruptly— as on a child's first day of school, graduation, marriage, and retirement—but generally the self is ultraconservative. As Lecky (1945) reported, the self resists change and strives for consistency. This general tendency was illustrated by both Balester (1956) and Roth (1959), who found that most individuals possess a significant degree of consistency in self concept as measured by "Q Sort." (For a description of "Q Sort," please see Chapter 4.) A similar finding was reported by Engel (1959), who investigated the stability of the self over a two-year period of adolescence and found that the self resists modification to a surprising degree. Actually, this resistence to change is a positive feature. If the self varied much, the individual would lack a consistent personality. No matter how negative the self may be, *who and what he is* is most important to the person, and just about anything is better than no self at all.

So it is that the self resists change as much as possible in order to enjoy a consistent and organized world. However, the self will change if conditions are favorable. If the child sees the educative process as meaningful and self-enhancing, and if the degree of threat provided by the school experience is not over-powering, then he is likely to grow in self-esteem and in academic achievement. Very few students want to be failures at learning, just as few teachers want to be failures at teaching.

The self and motivation A final dynamic quality of the self is its role in motivation. As we have seen, Combs, Snygg and Rogers believe that the maintenance and enhancement of the perceived self is the motive behind all behavior. If this is so, then it follows that there is only one kind of motivation, and that is the personal, internal motivation that each and every human being has at all times, in all places, and when engaged in any activity. As Combs has stated, "[P]eople are always motivated; in fact, they are never unmotivated. They may not be motivated to do what we would prefer they do, but it can never be truly said that they are un-motivated" (1962b, pp. 85f). Again turning to Combs, we find a succinct statement of the nature of this motivation, which is "an insatiable need for the maintenance and enhancement of the self; not the physical self—but the phenomenal self, of which the individual is aware, his self concept" (1965b, p. 8). For the teacher, this is a given, basic drive toward self-fulfillment. It may be inherent or learned, but in either case it is present long before the child enters school. It is a built-in advantage for the teacher, for it is a force that comes from within each student. A further treatment of this concept of motivation may be found in Avila and Purkey (1966).

An important assumption of this book is that each individual is striving to behave in ways which are consistent with his self-interpretation. To put it another way, people are constantly trying to behave in a manner which is consistent with the way they view themselves. Festinger (1962, 1967) maintains that "dissonance" (an uncomfortable state of mind) results when we take action which is incompatible with the beliefs we hold about ourselves. The ways we react to people, tasks, and roles, therefore, are those which seem to us to be most consistent with our self-image. We express our self concept with our behavior. If a high-school boy chooses to construe himself as a "ladies' man," his behavior will very likely differ from that of the fellow who sees himself as unattractive to the opposite sex.

Conclusion

In this first chapter we have taken a brief look at the history of the concept of self and then considered some of its characteristics. Among the most important characteristics were: (1) that the self is organized and dynamic; (2) that to the experiencing individual the self is the center of his personal universe; (3) that everything is observed, interpreted, and comprehended from this personal vantage point; and (4) that human motivation is a product of the universal striving to maintain, protect, and enhance the self.

The world of the self may appear to the outsider to be subjective and hypothetical, but to the experiencing individual it has the feeling of absolute reality. Tennyson expressed it this way:

> I am a part of all that I have met
> Yet all experience is an arch where through
> Gleams that untraveled world whose margin fades
> Forever and forever when I move.
>
> Tennyson, *Ulysses*

chapter two

THE SELF AND ACADEMIC PERFORMANCE

Linus: Look Sally, when I cut this apple in half, I have two halves.
Sally: That's fractions!!! I can't do fractions!! Fractions are too hard!
Linus: (sighs) I certainly don't envy teachers their lot.
Charles Shulz, *Peanuts* Cartoon

For generations, wise teachers have sensed the significant and positive relationship between a student's concept of himself and his performance in school. They believed that the students who feel good about themselves and their abilities are the ones who are most likely to succeed. Conversely, it appeared that those who see themselves and their abilities in a negative fashion usually fail to achieve good grades. Academic success or failure appears to be as deeply rooted in concepts of the self as it is in measured mental ability, if not deeper. In fact, Brookover (1967) concluded, from his extensive research on self-image and achievement, that the assumption that human ability is the most important factor in achievement is questionable, and that the student's attitudes limit the level of his achievement in school.

A milestone in our understanding of the self was Wylie's *The Self-Concept: A Critical Survey of Pertinent Research Literature*, which appeared in 1961. In this comprehensive review of hundreds of studies, Wylie was optimistic about the possibilities of research into the self concept but pessimistic over the general quality of the work up to that time. While Wylie's review is an excellent guide to the work accomplished up to 1960, one limitation of her book is that few of the studies reviewed could properly be described as research into the self concept. On close analysis, most of the work reviewed proved to be studies of the self-report. The difference, in Combs's words, is that the self concept is "what an individual *believes* he is. The self report on the other hand, is what the subject is ready, willing, able or can be tricked to *say* he is. Clearly, these concepts are by no means the same" (1962a, p. 52). The difference between self-report and self concept is an important one, and is treated in some detail in Chapter 4. For now, as we consider the research accomplished since 1960, I will indicate when a study used the self-report as a way of exploring the self concept.

Since 1960 there has been a fresh and invigorating amount of research into the relationship between the self concept and academic achievement. The questions dealt with can be divided into three categories: (1) the relation between the self and success in school (2) how the successful student views himself; and (3) how the unsuccessful student sees himself.

THE RELATIONSHIP BETWEEN THE SELF CONCEPT AND SUCCESS IN SCHOOL

Over-all, the research evidence clearly shows a persistent and significant relationship between the self concept and academic achievement. This relationship appears quite clear for boys, but less so for girls. Both Campbell (1965) and Bledsoe (1967), using self-report inventories, found a stronger relationship between the self concept and achievement in boys than in girls. Sex differences do seem to influence the relationship between the self and achievement, primarily in the area of underachievement. Male underachievers tend to have more negative self concepts than female underachievers. The reason for this may perhaps be learned from a study by Baum et al. (1969), who found, through repeated testing with the *Self-Concept as Learner Scale*, a self-report inventory, that girls, both high and low achievers, report a higher self concept than boys, and that girls as a group, indicate higher self concepts. This question of the influence of sex on the self concept is a rich field of exploration and needs much more research.

In 1960, Shaw, Edson, and Bell conducted a study to determine differences between achievers' and underachievers' perceptions of themselves. Their method was to compare groups of achievers and underachievers selected from among high-school juniors and seniors. The *Sarbin Adjective Checklist* was administered to each subject in order to measure the perceived self. They reported that male achievers scored significantly higher than underachievers on the following adjectives: Realistic, Optimistic, Enthusiastic, Reliable, Clear-thinking, and Intelligent. Female achievers scored lower than underachievers on only two adjectives: Ambitious and Responsible. Female underachievers, however, scored higher than achievers on: Fussy, Confused, Hardheaded, Lovable, Moody, Jolly, Unselfish, Anxious, Mischievous, Kind, Pleasure-seeking, Softhearted, Easygoing, and Considerate. A major conclusion of the study was that male achievers feel relatively more positive about themselves than male underachievers. No simple generalization could be made about the female groups, where there seemed to be some contradictions in the adjectives checked.

A related study of the relationship between academic underachievement and self concept was done by Fink (1962), who studied two groups of ninth-grade students paired for achievement and underachievement. The self image of each student was judged as adequate or inadequate by three separate psychologists, on the basis of data from the *California Psychological Inventory*, the *Bender Visual-Motor Gestalt Test*, the *Draw-a-Person Test*, the *Gough Adjective Checklist*, a personal data sheet, and a student essay entitled "What I will be in 20 years."

The combined ratings of the three psychologists showed significant differences between achievers and underachievers, the achievers being rated as far more adequate in their concepts of themselves. Fink concluded that there is a significant relationship between self concept and academic underachievement, and that this relationship appears stronger in boys than girls.

In 1964, Brookover, Thomas and Patterson conducted a study which had three purposes: (1) to determine whether the student's concept of his ability in school is significantly and positively related to academic performance; (2) to see if the self concept is differentiated into specific self concepts which correspond to specific subject-matter areas; and (3) to see if the self concept is significantly and positively correlated with the student's perception of how significant others view his ability.

The method employed was to study the self reports of over 1,000 seventh-grade, white students in an urban school system. Each child was given the Self Concept of Ability scale, to determine his concept of his own ability, both in general and in particular subjects.

After the I.Q. was factored out, the students' reported concepts of their own ability and their grade-point averages were found to be significantly and positively correlated. Brookover and his associates concluded that the relationship is substantial even when measured I.Q. is controlled. Moreover, there are specific self concepts of ability which are related to specific academic areas and which differ from the self concept of general ability. Finally, the self concept is significantly and positively correlated with the perceived evaluations of the student by other significant people. In summarizing their 1964 research, Brookover, Paterson, and Thomas (1965) concluded that self concept of academic ability is associated with academic achievement at each grade level.

Since 1967 there have been numerous other studies which point to the significant relationship between self concept and academic achievement. Campbell (1967) reported a low positive correlation between the *Coopersmith Self-esteem Inventory*, a self-report questionnaire, and the achievement of fourth, fifth, and sixth-grade students. Bledsoe (1967) explored the relationship of the self concepts of fourth and sixth-grade children to their intelligence, achievement, interests, and anxiety, using the *Bledsoe Self Concept Scale*, and found significant correlations between the professed self concept and the achievement of boys, but insignificant correlations for girls. Also in 1967, Irwin studied the self reports of freshmen college students and reported significant relationships between reported self concept and academic achievement. He summarized his research by stating: "[I]t may well be that a positive conception of one's self as a person is not only more important than striving to get ahead and enthusiasm for studying and going to school, but that it is a central factor when considering optimal scholastic performance" (p. 271).

In a study of Negro students, Caplin (1966) found that children who professed more positive self concepts tended to have higher academic achievement. It appears that the influence of the self has no racial boundaries. Students who feel ill about their abilities seldom succeed in school, regardless of their color.

Finally, Gill found patterns of achievement significantly related to the perceived self in public-school students. He concluded his paper by stating: "The results of this study support the conclusion with such convincing uniformity that the importance of the self concept in the educational process seems to need more emphasis than is presently given to it" (1969, p. 6).

How the Successful Student Sees Himself

The conclusion that the successful student is one who is likely to see himself in essentially positive ways has been verified by a host of studies. In an early investigation of factors of achievement in high school and college, Gowan (1960) reported that achievers are characterized by self confidence, self acceptance, and a positive self concept. Brunkan and Sheni (1966) considered effective and ineffective readers at the college level and found that the efficient and effective readers characterized themselves in favorable ways, which was not true of the ineffective readers. Farls (1967) studied intermediate-grade students and found that high-achieving boys and girls reported significantly higher self concepts in general and self concepts as students than low-achieving boys and girls. Also in 1967, Davidson and Greenberg investigated successful learners among lower-class children and the correlates of school achievement within this group. On three different and distinct aspects of the self—Personal competence, Academic competence, and Social competence—the high achievers rated themselves significantly better than did the low achievers. In a similar study, Williams and Cole (1968) explored the relationship between the reported self concepts and school adjustment of 80 sixth-grade students, and found significant positive correlations between their self concepts and such variables as reading and mathematical achievement. Still another study relating self report to achievement was accomplished by Farquhar (1968), who studied eleventh-grade high-school students. His study showed that over and underachievers respond with significant differences to items designed to measure their reflected self concept, and that students with high academic productivity tended to have high self concepts.

In an extensive research project which we have already mentioned, Brookover and his associates completed three projects (1962 through 1968) which represented continuous phases of a six-year study of the relation of the self concept of academic ability to school achievement among students in one school class while in the seventh through the twelfth grades. Among their findings were that the reported self concept of ability is significantly related to achievement among both boys and girls, that this relationship persists even when intelligence is factored out, that achievement in school is limited by the student's concept of his ability, and that the self concept of ability is a better predictor of success in school than is over-all self concept.

One interesting finding of the Brookover studies is that while students who report low self concepts rarely perform at above-average levels, as would be expected, a significant proportion of those who profess high self concepts of ability, surprisingly, do not perform at comparable levels. This led Brookover to hypothesize that confidence in one's academic ability is a necessary, but not sufficient, factor in determining scholastic success.

Why some students with high self concepts of ability fail to succeed in school remains to be explored, but it can be conjectured that there are students, particularly among the socially disabled, who believe that they have the ability to succeed in school but who view school as irrelevant, threatening, or both. The finding that socially disabled students do not necessarily report low self concepts is borne out by a study by Soares and Soares (1969), who completed a comparative study of the self-perceptions of disadvantaged and advantaged elementary-school children and found on the whole, more positive self-perceptions among the disadvantaged than the advantaged children. Other studies which question the commonly held assumption that disadvantaged children have negative self concepts include those of Kerensky (1967) and Carter (1968). Judging by the available evidence, it seems hazardous to assume that ghetto children, because of their socioeconomic circumstances, have lower self concepts than children in better environments. The causes of negative self concepts, as we shall see in the next chapter, are more psychological than economic.

A composite portrait of the successful student would seem to show that he has a relatively high opinion of himself and is optimistic about his future performance (Ringness, 1961). He has confidence in his general ability (Taylor, 1964) and in his ability as a student (Brookover, 1969). He needs fewer favorable evaluations from others (Dittes, 1959), and he feels that he works hard, is liked by other students and is generally polite and honest (Davidson and Greenberg, 1967). Judging by their statements, successful students can generally be characterized as having positive self concepts and tending to excel in feelings of worth as individuals. This is in stark contrast to the self-image of the majority of unsuccessful students, as we shall see.

How the Unsuccessful Student Sees Himself

> A person who doubts himself is like a
> man who would enlist in the ranks of
> his enemies and bear arms against himself.
> He makes his failure certain by himself being
> the first person to be convinced of it.
>
> *Alexandre Dumas.*

It is a personal tragedy and a social waste when a student spends year after year experiencing defeat and failure in school. The causes of the failure and the effects of the failing experience are complex, but a continuous and central factor in both cause and effect is the way in which a student views himself and his abilities.

Most studies dealing with the unsuccessful student have focused on the problem of underachievement, the "underachiever" being one whose classroom performance tends to be below his demonstrated aptitudes as measured by mental ability tests. In other words, he is the student who has the ability to succeed in school but who, because of nonintellectual factors, does not perform up to expectations. Fewer studies have considered the "nonachiever," the one who lacks the ability to meet the demands of school. But there is ample evidence to support the conclusion that unsuccessful students in either group perceive themselves and their relationships to the world around them differently than those who succeed.

Studies which support the notion that underachievers tend to have negative self concepts are numerous. In 1960, Goldberg studied underachievers in grades 9 through 12. On a list of characteristics and abilities called How I Am, the underachiever was found to perceive himself as less able to fulfill required tasks, less eager to learn, less confident, and less ambitious. In the following year Shaw (1961) reported that underachievers have a more negative self concept than achievers and demonstrate less mature behavior than achieving peers. This tendency toward immaturity of behavior was also reported by Bruck and Bodwin (1962), who studied students from grades 3, 6, and 11 and found a positive relationship between educational disability and immature self concept as measured by the Self Concept Scale of the Machover *Draw-A-Person Test.*

In 1963, Shaw and Alves attempted to verify previous findings (Shaw, Edison & Bell, 1960) that bright, underachieving, male high-school students have more negative self concepts than equally bright, achieving male students. Their results showed that male achievers and underachievers reported significant differences on the variables of Self concept, Self acceptance, and the Self acceptance of peers. They concluded that their study confirmed the results of the previous one: that male underachievers have more negative self concepts than achievers. In addition, the 1963 study showed that male underachievers were less self-accepting and attributed a similar lack of self-acceptance to their peers. Underachieving females in the study had ambivalent self concepts.

More recent studies seem to confirm the finding of earlier ones that underachievers generally see themselves as less adequate and less accepted by others. Combs (1963) studied the relationship between self-perceptions and underachievement in high-school boys and found that underachievers see themselves as less adequate and less acceptable to others, and that they find their peers and adults less acceptable. Durr and Schmatz (1964) investigated differences between achieving and underachieving elementary-school children, and reported that underachievers were more withdrawing, and tended to lack self-reliance, a sense of personal worth, and a feeling of belonging. They also reported finding behavioral immaturity and feelings of inadequacy.

Taylor's 1964 review of the literature on personality traits and discrepant achievement reported research findings that the underachiever is, among other things, self-derogatory, has a depressed attitude toward himself, has feelings of inadequacy, and tends to have strong inferiority feelings. One study reviewed by Taylor which did not confirm the general theory of the negative self-evaluation of unsuccessful students was that of Holland (1959), who found that the underachievers in his study tended to have positive self concepts. However, most investigators agree that the underachieving student sees himself as less capable, less worthy, and less adequate than his more successful peers.

The available information on the nonachiever suggests that he also holds unflattering views about himself. The nonachiever is in the unenviable position of lacking the ability to meet the demands of school, so that he must, unless the school makes special arrangements for him, face repeated failure. A comparative study by Harding (1966) of Caucasian, male, high-school students who stay in school and those who drop out found that the dropouts have significantly lower self concepts of their academic ability, when I.Q. and grade-point averages were factored out. Harding concluded that a student's attitude toward his ability to achieve in academic endeavors is a critical variable in predicting whether the student will continue in school or whether he will drop out.

Finally, there is growing evidence that poor reading ability is closely bound up with feelings of personal worth. Zimmerman and Allebrand (1965) studied urban fourth and fifth-graders of middle to lower socioeconomic status, half of Mexican descent, and found that poor readers, according to their performance on the *California Test of Personality*, a self-report inventory, lacked sufficient sense of personal worth, freedom, stability, and adequacy—to the extent that they avoided achievement. Carlton and Moore (1966, 1968) also have given heavy emphasis to the importance of the self concept to reading ability. They have shown that self-directed dramatization and self-selection of stories can improve the reading skills of elementary-school children while bringing about favorable changes in their professed self concepts.

Judging by the preponderance of available research, it seems reasonable to assume that unsuccessful students, whether underachievers, nonachievers, or poor readers, are likely to hold attitudes about themselves and their abilities which are pervasively negative. They tend to see themselves as less able, less adequate, and less self-reliant than their more successful peers. This is particularly true of boys, and it is also true, but to a lesser extent, of girls. Students with negative self-images of ability rarely perform well in school, as the research of Brookover, Erickson, and Joiner (1967) has indicated. Of even more sinister significance, continued feelings of worthlessness are, as Fromm (1941, 1947) points out, a characteristic of the unhealthy personality. The basic question of whether children see themselves negatively because of their poor school performance, or whether they perform poorly in school because they see themselves negatively, is unresolved. However, there is some research which pertains to this question of cause and effect as we shall see.

CAUSE AND EFFECT

Judging by the studies considered thus far, there is no question that there is a persistent relationship between the self and academic achievement. However, a great deal of caution is needed before one assumes that either the self concept determines scholastic performance or that scholastic performance shapes the self concept. It may be that the relationship between the two is caused by some factor yet to be determined. The best evidence now available suggests that it is a two-way street, that there is a continuous interaction between the self and academic achievement, and that each directly influences the other.

The Self Concept Influences Performance

There is little professional argument with the common-sense notion that our thoughts influence our behavior. Once we have acquired an idea about ourselves, it serves to edit all incoming information and to influence our future performance. Several studies have concluded that self concepts stand in a causal relationship to academic achievement.

In an investigation of the relationship between children's perceptions of themselves and their world while in kindergarten and their subsequent achievement in reading in the first grade, Lamy (1965) found that these perceptions, obtained from inferences made by trained observers, gave as good a prediction of later reading achievement as intelligence test scores. When I.Q. and self-evaluations were combined, the predictive power was even greater. In concluding her study, Lamy suggested that the perceptions of a child about himself and his world are not only related to, but may in fact be causal factors in, his subsequent reading achievement.

A similar study was done by Wattenberg and Clifford (1964).

They obtained measures of the self concepts of kindergarten children based on self-referent statements obtained as the children drew pictures of their family and as they responded to incomplete sentences. The scores obtained by the researchers were seen as representing two dimensions of the self concept: competence and goodness. These scores were then related to beginning achievement in reading during the second grade. The results indicated that measures of the self concept appear to be antecedent to and predictive of reading achievement in the second grade.

Other studies have pointed to the value of attitudes toward the self in the prediction of future performance in school. Benjamins (1950) reported that when the individual's self is influenced, changed, or threatened, it is reflected in his overt behavior. Bieri and Trieschman (1956) concluded that the self concept may influence certain aspects of social learning. Barrett (1957), in his study of gifted children, reported that feelings of inadequacy among bright underachievers act as depressors which cause them to withdraw and refuse to compete. Morse (1963) found that the reported self concept of ability was a better predictor of classroom achievement than I.Q., and that this was true for both Negro and Caucasian students. Haarer (1964) worked with ninth-graders and found that the reported self concept of ability was better than the I.Q. as a predictor of the achievement of both public-school male students and institutionalized delinquent boys. Brookover and his associates (1962, 1965) concluded from their studies that changes in the professed self concept of academic ability are associated with parallel changes in academic achievement. Harding (1966) reported that attitudes toward their own ability to achieve in academic endeavors was an essential factor in predicting whether high-school students would or would not quit schoool. Keefer (1966), in studying self-predictions of academic achievement by college students, found they were better predictors of collegiate achievement than high-school grades and American College Test scores, and that they lost less predictive accuracy after the freshman year than did the more traditional measures of grades and achievement test scores. Finally, Ludwig and Maehr (1967) found that professed changes in the self concept result in changes in preference and choice among junior high school boys.

The conclusion seems unavoidable: a student carries with him certain attitudes about himself and his abilities which play a primary role in how he performs in school. Yet as we have seen, the sword cuts both ways. Scholastic performance has a heavy impact on the self concept.

Performance Influences the Self Concept

A number of researchers, (Diller, 1954; Stotland and Zander, 1958; Borislow, 1962; and Dyson, 1967) have explored the conditions under which success and failure affect a person's evaluations of himself. There is general agreement among researchers with the common-sense view that students who underachieve scholastically, or who fail to live up to their own academic expectations, suffer significant losses in self-esteem. An example of this type of study is that of Gibby and Gibby (1967); who explored the effects of stress induced by academic failure upon seventh-grade students.

The researchers hypothesized that children would react to failure in an area considered by them to be important by manifesting a lowered opinion of themselves and their abilities. They further hypothesized that the children would feel that the significant persons in their lives would think less highly of them following such a failing experience. The study explored two broad aspects of the effects of stress resulting from failure: (1) the effects upon the self concept; and (2) the effects upon intellectual productivity.

For their subjects, Gibby and Gibby selected 60 students in two seventh-grade classes established for bright and academically superior white children. None had ever failed in school and all were aware of their special academic placement and superior abilities. One class was utilized as the control group and the other as the experimental group. Both groups were then administered three tests: an English grammar test, the Gibby Intelligence Rating Schedule, and a test of word fluency. Three days later, both groups were again given the test of word fluency, but just before the testing, members of the experimental group received slips of paper indicating that they had failed the previous test. The scores of the experimental and control groups on the test were then compared.

The results indicated that, under the stress of the failure situation, able children performed less effectively. Further, as shown by self-referent statements children in the experimental group tended to regard themselves less highly, tended to believe that they were not as highly regarded by significant others in their lives, and showed a decrement in intellectual productivity. The negative effect of failure was manifested in both the reported self concept and the measured cognitive function.

The tendency to acquire a lower general self-evaluation following failure appears to be as true of the underachiever as it is for the achiever. Centi (1965) reported a very strong pattern of such behavior among low achievers. He studied the self-reports of college freshmen before school began and after receiving their first-semester grades. Students who received poor grades suffered losses of self-esteem. They then began to rationalize their performance. Finally, they began to show hostility and dissatisfaction, first with the course, then with the teacher, and finally with the school and their classmates. They ultimately avoided study and devoted their time to other activities, causing a further decline in their academic achievement.

Just as poor performance lowers self-regard, successful performance raises it. In their study of reading which we mentioned earlier, Carlton and Moore (1966, 1968) allowed culturally disadvantaged children to select and dramatize stories. They found significant changes in the self concepts of their subjects, as well as improved reading ability, and reported that the changes in self concept were relatively permanent. This study seems to echo earlier studies by Diller (1954), who worked with college students and found that success enhanced their self concept, and by Bills (1959), who reported positive changes in children's self concepts as a result of nondirective play therapy.

The indications seem to be that success or failure in school significantly influence the ways in which students view themselves. Students who experience repeated success in school are likely to develop positive feelings about their abilities, while those who encounter failure tend to develop negative views of themselves. In the light of the influence of the self concept on academic achievement, it would seem like a good idea for schools to follow the precept I saw printed on an automobile drag-strip racing program: "Every effort is made to insure that each entry has a reasonable chance of victory."

CONCLUSION

In this chapter we have seen that there is a persistent and significant relationship between the self concept and academic achievement at each grade level, and that change in one seems to be associated with change in the other. Studies have been presented to indicate how the successful student sees himself, and how his self concept contrasts with the self-image of the failing student. Although the data do not provide clear-cut evidence about which comes first—a positive self concept or scholastic success, a negative self concept or scholastic failure— it does stress a strong reciprocal relationship and gives us reason to assume that enhancing the self concept is a vital influence in improving academic performance. Following up the implications of this assumption, we will consider in Chapter 3, the beginnings of the self and what happens under the impact of school. In Chapter 4 we will point out what the teacher can do to build positive and realistic self concepts in his students.

chapter three

GROWTH OF THE SELF

First was the golden age . . .
Where all were content.
When food came of itself . . .
And spring was everlasting.
Then did mild and sweet nectar
Flow for all.

Ovid, *Metamorphoses*

The self is acquired and modified through the accumulated experiences of the emerging individual. This miraculous accomplishment has been pictured by numerous writers and researchers, among the most graphic accounts being those of Cooley (1902), Mead (1934), Sullivan (1947), Jersild (1952), Block (1952), Farber (1962), Kelly (1962a), Goldstein (1963), and Coopersmith (1967). From the information provided by these and other writers, we can prepare a brief overview of the fires of experience which create self.

Self-awareness is a basic human condition which emerges during the early months of life. Gradually, the infant begins to recognize the presence of significant others which sets the stage for the beginnings of awareness of self as an independent agent. The child, like Walt Whitman's *Noiseless Patient Spider*, begins to launch forth filament, filament, filament to explore the "vacant, vast surrounding." (1948)

BEGINNINGS OF THE SELF

For the potential of the oak lies vibrating within the atomic structure of the acorn, as does the flower live within the bud and the Self within man.

Master Subramuniya, *Cognizantability*

As far as we can tell, the newborn baby is unaware of his existence as a unique and separate entity. But as the days pass he experiences continuous changes in his internal and external environments. Through layer after layer of direct experience with smells, sights, sounds, tastes, feelings, and pressures, he begins to organize a coherent mental organization of his world and to adapt to the external environment. It is this cauldron of experience, this process of mental organization and adaptation, which forges the self.

In the beginning of his relatively independent life, the newborn child is rudely ejected from a warm womb into a world of myriad sensations. Just getting born is a hectic experience. The infant makes his first appearance to the light of day red and crumpled, with shoulders hunched and head elongated. He has come through a pretty battering experience and his face looks like that of a boxer after a hard fight. With his first breaths, the infant begins the arduous and lifelong process of ordering and mastering his new environment. "There was a child went forth," as Walt Whitman named his poem, "and the first object he look'd upon, that object he became." (1948)

In his treatment of motivation, White (1959) has suggested that from infancy onward the child obtains a biologically given sense of pleasure from becoming competent in mastering the environment. This feeling of competence, according to White, is a source of satisfaction to the child which is independent of extrinsic rewards, punishments, or social expectancy. This fits in nicely with the concept of motivation presented in Chapter 1, that every child is *intrinsically* motivated to achieve further and greater control over his world by reason of the innate sources of satisfaction that accompany mastery of the environment. From the newborn baby's activities, it would appear that the concept of intrinsic motivation, presented by Combs, by Rogers and by White, is correct.

Within seconds after birth, with his first gasps, the child is beginning to use his new environment. As Ames (1952) indicates, the infant soon begins to develop and practice tiny patterns of action and perception. Within weeks he is organizing more complex patterns of behavior and training his eyes to follow objects accurately, as well as giving definite heed to sounds. Already he has acquired differentiated cries for discomfort, pain, and hunger. By the time he is several months old he holds his head erect for a short time when held to the shoulder. Soon he begins to repeat acts which produce interesting results, such as kicking his legs to make a bell vibrate. Also, at this early age, he starts to realize that certain events occur together and that certain others recur on a regular schedule. Shortly he begins to associate these events and learns that handling by an adult is associated with the pleasure of feeding.

By the time a baby is a few months old, he is deliberately responding to other people, smiling at their faces and even vocalizing at his own reflection in a mirror. He smiles and coos and delights in imitating the familiar (e.g., working saliva in one's mouth will usually bring a similar response from a three- or four-month old infant). Already he is flinging his hands toward dangled objects, and he is learning to reach and grasp so that he can investigate the world more fully.

Long before his first birthday, the baby has learned a tremendous amount about the world in which he lives. He knows what many objects look and feel like, what they can do, and what their value is to him. He has slid slippery things through his hands, he has stuck his fingers in holes, he has tasted everything he could put his mouth to, he has dropped things to watch them fall, and he has splashed water to enjoy the spray.

During this first year of life the baby has learned many things about himself. He has learned to discriminate the "me" from the "not me" and to attribute intention to the acts of others. He is now aware of the major parts of his body and how they relate to each other, and he has found boundaries between his body and the outside world. Most importantly, he has begun to sense his value and worth as a human being: He is well on his way to creating a self. As Sigel and Hooper (1968) note, the formation of the self is a special manifestation of a general human need to determine certain constancies from the world of continuous sensation.

Because the self is not instinctive, but is developed as a process of experience, it is remarkably plastic, changeable, and possesses infinite capacity for growth and actualization. The main forces which shape the self are significant others. Self-evaluation, as Helper (1958) indicates, arrives rather directly from the evaluations made of the individual by others. It is difficult to overestimate the impact of significant others in the early environment in which the child finds himself, as we shall see.

THE EARLY ENVIRONMENT

Speak roughly to your little boy
And beat him when he sneezes,
He only does it to annoy
Because he knows it teases.

Lewis Carroll, *Alice in Wonderland*

Sometime in the first year of life, much earlier than most parents would believe possible, the infant has developed a myriad number of perceptions about himself, thoughts and feelings which make up his awareness of his individual existence. Psychologists call these perceptions his "self concept", but to the child it's simply who and what he is. After he begins talking, he will speak of these perceptions as simply "me."

During the early months of life the infant is utterly dependent upon the love and care of those responsible for him. The nature of this love and care has an overwhelming influence on the way the infant sees himself and the world. If the child's experiences with important people in his life are good, and if he is accepted unconditionally, then he can begin to expand as a person. The development of his capacity to love is facilitated by his being loved and by being surrounded by people who love each other. His intelligence is increased by being exposed to an enriched and varied perceptual environment. His emerging self is enhanced by treatment which tells him that he is wanted, liked, valued, healthy—in other words, a "good" baby. For good or ill, the child is molded by the repeated behavior of the significant people in his life.

As you would expect, the parents are the ones who reflect the earliest appraisals. They determine the child's environment by giving or withholding love and affection, rewards and punishments, and by serving as models and examples. The mother is in a particularly strategic position. Through the presence or absence of her smiling, kissing, nuzzling, rubbing, tasting, playing, and all the rest of mothering behavior, she tells the baby how wonderful and wanted, or disgusting and unwanted, he is. Also, as studies by Symonds (1939), Farber (1962), and others point out, the mother is not only vital in providing support and acceptance of the child, she also serves as a model for her daughters and determines the stature of the father as a masculine model for the son.

Together, the mother and father are critical in molding and maintaining the child's self-image. Manis (1958) reported from his research that a child's level of self-regard is closely associated with his parents' reported level of regard for him. Similar findings by Davidson and Lang (1960), Shaw and Dutton (1965), Brookover et al. (1965), and Meyers (1966) strongly suggest that a child's behavior is a function of the expectations of others who are significant to him. In other words, the expectations of significant others are internalized into self-perceptions.

Joan Anglund (1964) wrote that childhood is the happy hour, the tender time of innocence. Unfortunately, many children live in a nightmare. They are psychologically crippled and pauperized by inadequate love and care. Redl and Wineman, in their study of children who hate, reported that in their subjects "the quality of the tie between child and adult world was marred by rejection ranging from open brutality, cruelty, and neglect to affect barrenness on the part of some parents and narcissistic absorption in their own interests which exiled the child emotionally from them" (1952). Although ignorant and sadistic parents abound, this crippling of children by adults is usually not done on purpose. Few parents want to be failures at raising children, just as few teachers want to fail as teachers and few psychologists want to fail as psychologists. Yet through lack of knowledge, or insensitivity, or because of a history which they are now recreating by the pattern in which they rear their own children, they cripple their children. This syndrome of recreating childhood abuses was recognized as early as 1939 by Symonds, and is a recurring finding of research in the psychology of parent-child relationships. The crippling process might be compared by analogy to the older Chinese practice of foot binding. In earlier China, mothers would tightly bind their young daughters' feet and keep them bound for years, causing terrible deformity. It was done with good intent, because tiny feet and a mincing walk were considered attractive in a Chinese girl. In time, the crippled daughter would grow up, marry, and have daughters of her own. Then the irony:

the crippled mother would get out the bandages and cripple her daughters just as she was crippled. Through generation after generation, like echoes in a canyon, the crippling continued. An old Russian proverb states the problem succinctly: "The little girl who is beaten will beat her doll-baby." We do unto others as we have been done unto.

So it happens that many small children are crippled by parents who were themselves crippled psychologically as children. As Block noted, "when parents are overburdened by their inadequacies, any additional demands by children produce intolerable anxiety. In many cases the slightest indication of a wish for some sort of satisfaction brings down a rain of blows, either psychic or physical, upon the child's head" (1952, p. 298). Many children's capacity to love is permanently inhibited because important people fail to provide warmth and affection when it is needed most. Their intellectual development is stultified because they are reared in a deprived and sterile atmosphere. Their selves are hobbled, distorted, and defeated because participation with the meaningful people in their lives has given meanings to the self which are pervasively derogatory. Children are bent down by significant people in their lives, much like the birches, victims of ice storms, pictured by Robert Frost.

> When I see birches bent to right and left
> Across the line of straighter darker trees,
> I like to think some boy's been swinging them.
> But swinging doesn't bend them down to stay.
> Ice storms do that.....
>   Once they are bowed.
> So low for so long, they never right themselves.

As a general rule, we can say that any behavior of significant people that causes a young child to think ill of himself, to feel inadequate, incapable, unworthy, unwanted, unloved, or unable, is crippling to the self. Where respect and warmth are missing, where the child's questions go unanswered, where his offers to help are rejected, where his discipline is based on failure and punishment, where he is excluded from his parents' emotional life, and where his basic rights are abused, there his self is undermined. It is vital for parents to remember the simple rule that they must have respect for and confidence in their children before their children can have self-respect or self-confidence.

A poignant paradox is that sometimes the very desire to be a good mother or father will lead the parent to mistake duty for love. The parent thinks "I'm doing this for your own good" when he is excessively critical of the child, pointing out every mistake and picturing it as a child's personal failure. Children of such parents begin to question themselves and their abilities, to see themselves as failures and incompetents. Other parents, insecure and fearful themselves, become overprotective. They try to shield their children from every danger, real or imagined, near or remote. The child is taught that the world is filled with dangerous snakes, people, sickness, germs, death, falls, spiders, injuries, dogs, darkness, plants, sharp objects, water, and other dangers which the child cannot possibly face alone. With the best of intentions, parents give their children false and misleading perceptions of themselves and the world which deeply affects all future learning.

So it happens that the early years of life are most critical in forming the child's opinion of himself. The self is formed from the experience woven in everyday life, concealed in everyday occurrences, hidden in the deep communications of unspoken feelings and affection. The child becomes the way he is treated. W. Somerset Maugham expressed it beautifully in *The Razor's Edge*:

> For men and women are not only themselves; they are also the region in which they were born, the city apartment or the farm in which they learned to walk, the games they played as children, the old wives' tale they overheard, the food they ate, the schools they attended, the sports they followed, the poems they read, and the God they believed in.

By two-and-a-half years of age, the child is using the personal pronoun "I," but long before that the self, for better or worse, has been formed as the child defines his relationship with the significant people of his life. Fortunately, there are some clues to child rearing which we can examine briefly.

THE ENHANCING HOME ENVIRONMENT

Successful students, as we have seen, may generally be characterized as standing high in their own self-regard and as possessing confidence in their ability to cope successfully with life. Because of this persistent relationship between the self and scholastic success, it is helpful to explore briefly the characteristics of the enhancing home environment.

Judging by the available research (Brookover et al., 1965; Thomas, 1966; Coopersmith, 1967) as well as by everyday experience, there is little room for doubt that parents play an extremely vital role in the development of self-regard in their children. For example, in their attempts to improve scholastic achievement by enhancing students' self concept, Brookover et al. attempted three methods of treating 49 low-achieving ninth-grade students over a period of nine months: (1) to enhance the academic expectations and the evaluations his parents had of the student's ability; (2) to introduce the student to an "expert" who directly communicated enhancing information about his ability; and (3) to create a "significant other" in the form of a counselor whose high academic expectations and evaluations of the student might be internalized by him. Of the three approaches, only the first produced the desired results. When the perceptions of the parents were modified, the students changed their self-perception positively and also improved their grades, although the improvement was not maintained when the treatment was discontinued. It can be concluded from this study that the student's self-regard is much influenced by his parents' level of regard for him and his abilities.

A second interesting finding was that the parents' influence continues through the adolescent years. Parents were consistently ranked high as "significant others" by the subjects in Brookover's study, in contradiction to the common belief that the influence of parents declines during adolescence. Parents have a more vital and continuing role in the self-perceptions of their children than is generally recognized.

The research which has given us the clearest picture to date of the enhancing home environment is that reported by Coopersmith in *The Antecedents of Self-esteem* (1967). Coopersmith lists three conditions which lead the developing individual to value himself and to regard himself as an object of worth. These are (1) *parental warmth*, whereby the child senses the love and concern of his family and feels that they see him as a person of value; (2) *respectful treatment*, whereby the child's views are considered and where he has a rightful and democratic position in the family; and (3) *clearly defined limits*, whereby the child comes to know, through his parents' relatively high demands and expectations for success, that they care what happens to him. Together, these three conditions make up a generally prevailing parental attitude of positive regard and affection.

Surprisingly, the following factors do not appear to be associated with the formation of high self-esteem: amount of punishment, amount of time spent with parents, physical attractiveness, height, education, income, or even social class or ethnic background (Coopersmith, 1969). This last point, which relates to the self-esteem of culturally disadvantaged children, needs to be explored more fully. Ausubel and Ausubel (1963), Crovetto, Fischer and Boudreaux (1967), and Hawk (1967) all reported that the professed self concepts of disadvantaged children are characterized by low self-esteem and self-deprecation. However, Soares and Soares (1969), who conducted a comparative study of the self-perceptions of disadvantaged children and those of advantaged children in grades 4 to 8 of a New England city's elementary-school system, reported generally more positive self-perceptions for disadvantaged children than advantaged children. As we saw in Chapter 2, it is likely that the emotional climate of the family is more important than economic or social factors and that the emotional press toward low self-esteem can exist in both advantaged and disadvantaged families.

The critical factor is how the child interprets his parents' views of him. If parents wish to provide a home environment which will build positive self-regard in children, then they must give consideration to the attitudes they express toward their children and be sensitive to how these attitudes are being perceived.

ENTERING SCHOOL

Children come to school for the first time with a predisposition toward achievement or underachievement. Long before the first schoolbell rings, many children, particularly males, are oriented toward either success or failure in school. This assumption is supported by the research of Shaw and McCuen (1960) who attempted to determine the onset of academic underachievement in bright children. They concluded that in male underachievers, at least, the predisposition to underachieve was present when they entered school. In females, such predisposition could not be ruled out.

It is evident that children come to school with all sorts of ideas about themselves and their abilities. They have formed pictures of their value as human beings and of their ability to cope successfully with their environment. Like an invisible price tag, the child's self-image is with him wherever he goes, influencing whatever he does. For some children, the tag reads: "Damaged goods." For others, it may read "A fine value," or "An excellent buy," or even "Top value, one of a kind." Unfortunately, many read "Soiled, marked down" or "Close out, half price." Each of these tags is a social product given to children by the significant people in their lives. Some children enter school with the feeling that they are helpless, unable to cope. Others enter already carefully calibrated, their tag reads "Highly accurate," and they respond carefully to classroom instructions. For still other children the opposite is true, for they have never been encouraged to be careful, accurate, neat, or even honest.

When the invisible price tag is negative, it is probably more destructive than a physical handicap, for even the most insensitive parent or teacher can usually recognize and take into account a crippling physical handicap. Negative self-esteem, however, is often overlooked because we fail to take the time and effort it requires to be sensitive to how children see themselves and their abilities.

So it happens that children walk into class the first day of school with tags that read "Unworthy person," "Unsafe with people," "Physically weak," and "Generally unwanted and unliked." Morgan presents a vivid picture of how these attitudes toward oneself are related to antisocial behavior.

In a study completed at the University of Florida in 1961, Morgan compared the self-perceptions of aggressive children with those of withdrawn children, to determine whether there are differences in the perceived self of children who are aggressive at school as opposed to those who are withdrawn. Morgan assumed that, while both types of children present classroom problems, the aggressive ones would have more adequate self concepts and greater general intelligence.

Fifteen aggressive and fifteen withdrawn children were selected from referrals to the office of a school psychologist. They were chosen on the basis of comments of teachers, observations of each student in the classroom, and a test administered by the school psychologist. The classification of the student's behavior as predominantly aggressive or withdrawn was then confirmed by three other psychologists, and each child was given extensive testing which included both measures of intelligence and measures of attitudes toward the self.

Morgan found that the two groups did not vary significantly in intelligence, but that, as predicted, the total self concept scores were significantly higher for the aggressive children, as were the subscores having to do with how the aggressive child saw himself in relation to others, how he saw himself in relation to school, and whether he felt free to accomplish his own goals. All the children, in both groups, saw themselves as "unliked by people." Over half of the students in each group saw themselves as "unwanted by or unacceptable to people," "threatened by external environment," and "an unworthy person." The members of the aggressive group saw themselves as physically strong and as "able to assert oneself," while, as expected, the withdrawn group saw themselves as "unable to cope with people," "unsafe with people," and "physically weak." These responses were not found in the aggressive group.

Morgan concluded her study by stating that the most significantly different perception of the aggressive children was seeing themselves as "able to assert." The most significantly different perception of the withdrawn children was seeing themselves as "unable to cope" with people.

It appears that there is a close relationship between self-esteem (invisible price tags) and individual behavior. A study by Radke-Yarrow, Trager, and Davis (1949) shows that not only is there a connection between the self concept and behavior, but that in preschool and young school children there is awareness of racial and religious group membership which contribute an abasing or enhancing quality to the child's self concept.

Using elementary-school children, five to eight years of age, in kindergarten, first, and second grades, Radke-Yarrow, Trager, and Davis studied the early stages of social awareness and attitude development. Perceptions of and attitudes toward racial and religious groups were obtained from each child with the aid of a series of pictures (*Social Episodes Test*) which permit projections of content and of attitudes regarding racial and religious groups and which permit the examiner to probe aspects of attitudes. The pictures were of simple social situations, involving children on a playground, in a schoolroom, and on a city street. A major hypothesis was that group membership is a significant aspect of the self concept of children.

Many of the children interviewed indicated a sense of their own group membership, particularly of race. The researchers reported that children placed themselves in their own race and often attached an affective meaning to it. In addition, there was a competitive aspect to the affect: "I'm glad I belong to this group and not that group."

However, awareness of belonging to a particular *religious* group was not apparent in all children. Jewish children showed a greater awareness than either Catholic or Protestant. The investigators found that nonmembership in a group may be sensed by a child with as much import for his self-image as membership in a group: "I'm glad I'm not a Jew," or—as a Negro girl said in referring to a Negro child in a picture—"She wishes she were white."

The study demonstrates that group consciousness and social prejudices are present in the preschool and early school years, and highlights the dangers involved in assuming that group consciousness does not arise until adolescence or beyond. It further illustrates that the child's perceptions of his social environment do not occur independently of the development of his invisible price tags. A more recent study by Gabbler and Gibby (1967) tends to confirm Radke-Yarrow, Trager, and Davis, by revealing that Negro and white children differ significantly in self concept as measured by self-ratings of intelligence.

So it happens that the child enters school with his psychological bags packed with all sorts of ideas about himself and his abilities. However, in spite of this tremendous influence of the primary home environment, the school has a great role to play, as we shall see. Next to the home, the school is the single most important force in shaping the child's self concept.

THE SCHOOL ENVIRONMENT

> We all make mistakes. But to commit a wrong, to lower the dignity of a child and not be aware that the dignity has been impaired, is much more serious than the child's skipping of words during oral reading.
>
> C. Moustakas, *The Authentic Teacher*

Traditionally, the child is expected to adjust to the school, rather than the school adjusting to the child. To insure this process, the school is prepared to dispense rewards and punishments, successes and failures, on a massive scale. The child is expected to learn to live in a new environment and to compete for the rewards of obedience and scholarship. Schools stand ready with grades and grade-levels, report cards and honor rolls, continuous evaluation and fierce competition, detention centers and even expulsion, plus a host of other techniques to mold the child to meet the school's expectations. A sensitive and revealing account of life in the classroom is provided by Jackson (1968).

Unfortunately, a large number of schools employ a punitive approach to education. Punishment, failure, and deprecation are characteristic. In fact, Deutsch (1963) argues that it is often in the school that highly charged negative attitudes toward learning evolve. The principle that negative self concepts should be prevented is ignored by many schools.

All too often, schools are places where students face failure, rejection, and daily reminders of their limitations. Because some schools are unable to adjust themselves to individual differences of students (in spite of their written philosophies), untold children face daily deprecation and humiliation. The list of negative and punitive measures employed by well-meaning teachers provides good examples of the Procrustean bed of many schools.

Competitive evaluations, which ignore varying sociological backgrounds and individual differences in ability, often begin in the first grade and continue throughout school. "Grading on the curve" is popular, and competition among students is encouraged. Students are encouraged to enhance themselves by demonstrating their superiority over their fellow students. As Rosenberg points out:

> The general point is that whenever a value is set forth which can only be attained by a few, the conditions are ripe for widespread feelings of personal inadequacy. An outstanding example in American society is the fierce competitiveness of the school system. No educational system in the world has so many examinations, or so emphasized grades, as the American school system. Children are constantly being ranked and evaluated. The superior achievement of one child tends to debase the achievement of another (1965, pp. 281–82).

Many children give up early in school, feeling that with no attempt there can be little or no humiliation.

Another serious problem in American education is the policy of ability grouping, where children are graded by being placed in certain categories. While research is lacking, it may be *more* humiliating to be placed in "special classes" than to remain in the regular classroom and receive low grades. Certainly the process of sorting and labeling has been overdone, and can bring about all sorts of self-fulfilling prophecies, as Rosenthal and Jacobsen (1968a, b) have shown. A related problem is segregation, which operates so that students from minority groups, already socially handicapped, are excluded from learning social and civic skills in the one place still open to them, the school.

Other demeaning practices of schools would include retention, where children find themselves being "retained" for an entire year, and corporal punishment and related punitive techniques. While such practices have little or no support in research, they are widely practiced (Abramson, 1968). They are official policies in many schools, but there are also unofficial methods—scorn, sarcasm, and ridicule. From the child's point of view, schools can sometimes be the enemy, distributing failure and defeat to the very children who need to experience success the most. A study by Morse (1964) has shown how the school can instill negative feelings in the students.

To determine the value of the "Semantic Differential" (which measures dimensions of meanings) as a measure of self concept,

Morse measured the shifts in the self concept of elementary-school students. He administered the Semantic Differential to over 600 students in alternate grades, from grade 3 to 11, in a metropolitan school system. Analyzing the responses, Morse found a gradual decrease in professed self-regard with age. 84 per cent of the third-graders were proud of their work in school, compared to only 53 per cent of the eleventh graders. Similar findings were reported by Brookover et al. (1965) and Yamamoto, Thomas, and Karnes (1969).

What these studies seem to indicate is that the image of school grows gradually less positive with time, and communicates a sense of personal inadequacy to many students. If we are serious about making an understanding of self concept a central part of the school, then we must seek out ways of modifying our educational methods to prevent the development of negative self concepts in students. Teachers need to give serious application to learning the principles which call for a careful evaluation of present school policies in the light of what we know about the self and scholastic success. Once a child becomes convinced that school is not the place for him, that it is a place of threat and anxiety where he cannot hope to succeed and where his identity is lost, then the school as well as the student is in a very difficult position. In the next and final chapter, we shall consider the task of the teacher in overcoming negative influences and building positive and realistic self concepts in students.

chapter four

THE TASK
OF THE TEACHER

Let people realize clearly that every time they threaten someone or humiliate or hurt unnecessarily or dominate or reject another human being, they become forces for the creation of psychopathology, even if these be small forces. Let them recognize that every man who is kind, helpful, decent, psychologically democratic, affectionate, and warm, is a psychotherapeutic force even though a small one.
Abraham H. Maslow, *Motivation and Personality*

In this book you have been introduced to a body of theory about the self. We have considered some of the self's major characteristics, analyzed how the self and scholastic success are related, and reviewed the creation of the self. Now we turn our attention to the task of the teacher: to help each student gain a positive and realistic image of himself as a learner.

Before we consider the process of building positive and realistic self concepts in students, it is necessary to point out the need to avoid instilling negative ones. The self is remarkably conservative, and once a child has formed a negative image of himself as a learner, the task of the teacher becomes extremely difficult. Therefore, *the prevention of negative self concepts is a vital first step in teaching.* The unfavorable features of some schools, which we discussed in the previous chapter, can be modified by teachers who are aware of the need and who want to make changes.

Several studies have shown that it is possible to develop a curriculum in which the expected academic learning takes place while positive self concepts are being built. Frankel (1964) studied the effects of a special program of advanced summer study on the self-perceptions of academically talented high school students. He concluded that the self concepts of the group showed significant gains after attending the program, particularly in the areas of self-reliance and special talents. In a somewhat similar study of the effects of a pre-kindergarten on the self concept, Crovetto, Fischer, and Boudreaux (1967) developed a modified Head Start curriculum specifically designed to affect the child's self concept in a positive direction. When the experimental group of students was compared with a control group, it was found that the experimental class members showed gains on the *Draw-A-Man Test*, while the control group did not. The experimental curriculum appeared to be effective in helping to develop a more positive self concept in children.

Beneath program arrangements and curricular innovations lies the teacher's personal role. What part do teachers play in the development of the child's self? Can teachers change the child's self-image if they try to do so? If they can, what methods of teaching produce what kinds of self-image? Is it possible to distinguish between teachers in the frequency and kind of comment which they make about the child's self? To answer these questions, Staines (1958) conducted a study involving careful observation, recording, and analyzing of data from teacher-child and child-child interaction in four elementary school classrooms. Data were collected on the educational outcomes of the interaction between personalities in the atmosphere of the classroom, particular attention being given to identifying those teachers who could be reliably distinguished by the frequency of their use of words and kinds of situational management which, in the opinion of competent judges who served as observers, are likely to be positive influences on the self concepts of students.

The investigation showed marked differences between teachers in the frequency of references about the child in their comments, particularly in their positive or negative comments on the child's performance, status, and self-confidence or potency. Also, it was found that it is possible to teach so that, while aiming at the normal results of teaching, specific changes can be made in the child's self-image. Staines concluded that changes in the child's self concept do occur as an outcome of the learning situation, and that the self must be recognized as an important factor in learning. Teaching methods can be adapted so that definite changes of the kind sought for will occur in the self without injury to the academic program in the process.

Teachers want to be significant forces in the lives of their students. As Moustakas (1966) declared, every teacher wants to meet the student on a significant level, every teacher wants to feel that what he does makes a difference. Yet in order to influence students it is necessary to become a *significant other* in their lives. We are seldom changed by people whom we see as insignificant or unimportant. The way the teacher becomes significant seems to rest on two forces: (1) what he believes, and (2) what he does.

WHAT THE TEACHER BELIEVES

> No printed word nor spoken plea
> Can teach young minds what men should be,
> Not all the books on all the shelves
> But what the teachers are themselves.
>
> Anonymous

A basic assumption of the theory of the self concept is that we behave according to our beliefs. If this assumption is true, then it follows that the teacher's beliefs about himself and his students are crucial factors in determining his effectiveness in the classroom. Available evidence (Combs, 1969) indicates that the teacher's attitudes toward himself and others are as important, if not more so, than his techniques, practices, or materials. In fact, there do not seem to be any techniques which are always associated with people who are effective in the helping relationship. Rogers (1965) reported that personality changes in therapy come about not because of such factors as professional qualifications and training, or knowledge or skill, or ideological orientation, but primarily because of the attitudinal characteristics of the relationship. Attitudes play an important role, and so we need to examine the teacher's beliefs about himself and his students in some detail.

What the Teacher Believes About Himself

There seems to be general agreement that the teacher needs to have positive and realistic attitudes about himself and his abilities before he is able to reach out to like and respect others. Numerous studies (Berger, 1953; Fey, 1954; Luft, 1966) have reported that there is a marked relation between the way an individual sees himself and the way he sees others. Those who accept themselves tend to be more accepting of others (Trent, 1957) and perceive others as more accepting (Omwake, 1954). Further, according to Omwake, those who reject themselves hold a correspondingly low opinion of others and perceive others as being self-rejecting. From these studies it seems clear that the teacher needs to see himself in essentially positive ways. The manner in which this can be accomplished needs further investigation, but Jersild and Combs have given us some clues.

Jersild (1952, 1960, 1965) has been a pioneer in emphasizing the importance of the attitudes that teachers hold about themselves. He argues that the self-understanding of teachers is a necessary factor in coping with their feelings and in becoming more effective in the classroom. The personal problems of teachers often interfere with their effectiveness in teaching, and an understanding of the influence of these and other attitudes and emotions is vital in working with students. Jersild has suggested that we need to encourage in-service group counseling situations for teachers, in which their attitudes and feelings can be safely explored with others. This, it is hoped, would result in increased understanding of and sensitivity to oneself, and to more effective teaching in the classroom.

A similar view is reported by Combs and his associates (1963, 1964, 1965, 1969) in their research on the perceptual organization of effective helpers. They found that effective teachers, counselors, and priests could be distinguished from ineffective helpers on the basis of their attitudes about themselves and others. Such findings as these have long-range implications for the professional education of teachers. In fact, the suggestion that teacher preparation should be based on a perceptual, self concept approach has already appeared in Combs' The Professional Education of Teachers (1965), and an experimental program of teacher training using the perceptual approach was introduced at the University of Florida in 1969.

The way the evidence points is that each teacher needs to view himself with respect, liking, and acceptance. When teachers have essentially favorable attitudes toward themselves, they are in a much better position to build positive and realistic self concepts in their students.

What the Teacher Believes About Students

The ways significant others evaluate the student directly affects the student's conception of his academic ability. This in turn establishes limits on his success in school. Teachers, in their capacity of significant others, need to view students in essentially positive ways and hold favorable expectations. This is particularly important at the elementary level, but is vital in all grades. Several studies bear directly on the importance of what the teacher believes about students.

Davidson and Lang (1960) found that the student's perceptions of the teacher's feelings toward him correlated positively with his self-perception. Further, the more positive the children's perceptions of their teacher's feelings, the better their academic achievement and the more desirable their classroom behavior as rated by the teacher. Clarke (1960) reported a positive relationship between a student's academic performance and his perception of the academic expectations of him by significant others.

One of the most comprehensive studies of the self concept of ability and school success was that of Brookover and his associates (1965, 1967) which we considered, in part, earlier. Brookover and his associates conducted a six-year study of the relation between the self concept of academic ability and school achievement among students in one school class while in the seventh through the twelfth grades. A major purpose of the study was to determine whether improved self concept results from the expectations and evaluations held by significant others as perceived by the students. As Brookover, Erickson, and Joiner conclude: "The hypothesis that students' perceptions of the evaluations of their academic ability by others (teachers, parents, and friends) are associated with self concepts of academic ability was confirmed" (1967, p. 110). The almost unavoidable conclusion is that the teacher's attitudes and opinions regarding his students have a significant influence on their success in school. In other words, when the teacher believes that his students can achieve, the students appear to be more successful; when the teacher believes that the students cannot achieve, then it influences their performance negatively. This self-fulfilling prophecy has been illuminated by the research of Rosenthal and Jacobson (1968a, b).

The basic hypothesis of Rosenthal and Jacobson's research was that students, more often than not, do what is expected of them. To test this hypothesis, the two researchers conducted an experiment in a public elementary school of 650 students. The elementary-school teachers were told that, on the basis of ability tests administered the previous spring, approximately one-fifth of the students could be expected to evidence significant increases in mental ability during the year. The teachers were then given the names of the high-potential students. Although in fact the names had been *chosen at random* by the experimenters, when intelligence tests and other measures were administered some months later, those identified as potential spurters tended to score significantly higher than the children who had not been so identified. Also, Rosenthal and Jacobson found that these children were later described by their teachers as happier, more curious, more interesting, and as having a better chance of future success than other children. The conclusion drawn by Rosenthal and Jacobson is that the teacher, through his facial expressions, postures, and touch, through what, how, and when he spoke, subtly helped the child to learn. This may have been accomplished, according to the researchers, by modifying the child's self concept, his expectations of his own behavior, and his motivations, as well as his cognitive style. They summarized their study by stating that the evidence suggests strongly that "children who are expected by their teachers to gain intellectually in fact do show greater intellectual gains after one year than do children of whom such gains are not expected" (1968b, p. 121). The full educational implications of the self-fulfilling prophecy remain to be explored, but it seems certain that the ways the teacher views the student have a significant influence on the student and his performance.

WHAT THE TEACHER DOES

As we have seen, the key to building positive and realistic self-images in students lies largely in what the teacher *believes* about himself and his students. These beliefs not only determine the teacher's behavior, but are transmitted to the students and influence their performance as well. Yet we cannot ignore what the teacher *does* in the classroom, for the behavior he displays and the experiences he provides, *as perceived by students*, have a strong impact in themselves. In this section we will consider two important aspects of the teacher's role: (1) *the attitudes he conveys*; and (2) *the atmosphere he develops*.

The Attitude the Teacher Conveys

It is difficult to overestimate the need for the teacher to be sensitive to the attitudes he expresses toward students. Even though teachers may have the best intentions, they sometimes project distorted images of themselves. What a person believes can be hidden by negative habits picked up long ago. Therefore, teachers need to ask themselves:

Am I projecting an image that tells the student that I am here to build, rather than to destroy, him as a person? (Spaulding, 1963, reported that there is a significant relationship between a student's positive self concept as reported, and the degree to which teachers are calm, accepting, supportive, and facilitative, and a negative relationship between a student's self concept and teachers who are threatening, grim, and sarcastic.)

Do I let the student know that I am aware of and interested in him as a unique person? (Moustakas, 1966, maintains that every child wants to be known as a unique person, and that by holding the student in esteem, the teacher is establishing an environmental climate that facilitates growth.)

Do I convey my expectations and confidence that the student can accomplish work, can learn, and is competent? (Rosenthal and Jacobson, 1968b, have shown that the teacher's expectations have a significant influence on the student's performance.)

Do I provide well-defined standards of values, demands for competence, and guidance toward solutions to problems? (Coopersmith, 1967, has provided evidence that self-reliance is fostered by an environment which is well-structured and reasonably demanding, rather than unlimitedly permissive.)

When working with parents, do I enhance the academic expectations and evaluations which they hold of their children's ability? (Brookover, et al., 1965, has illustrated that this method yields significant results in enhancing self concept and improving academic achievement.)

By my behavior, do I serve as a model of authenticity for the student? (Both Jourard, 1964, and Rogers, 1965, suggest that a most important factor in the helping relationship is the helper serving as a model of genuineness, without "front.")

Do I take every opportunity to establish a high degree of private or semi-private communication with my students? (Spaulding, 1963, found a high relationship between the pupil's self concept and the teacher's behavior when it involved personal and private talks with students.)

The above questions are samples of how the teacher may check himself to see if he is conveying his beliefs in an authentic and meaningful fashion. As Gill reported, teachers' attitudes toward students are vitally important in shaping the self concepts of their students. Gill summarized his study by saying that "teachers should consider self concept as a vital and important aspect of learning and development which the school, through its educational process, should seek to promote and foster in every child" (1969, p. 10).

The Atmosphere the Teacher Creates

Six factors seem particularly important in creating a classroom atmosphere conducive to developing favorable self-images in students. These are (1) challenge; (2) freedom; (3) respect; (4) warmth; (5) control; and (6) success. A brief discussion of each of these may be helpful.

Challenge Because of the focus of this book, little has been said about high standards of academic accomplishment. This omission should not be taken to mean that achievement should be minimized. As we have seen, high academic expectations and a high degree of challenge on the part of teachers have a positive and beneficial effect on students. A good way to create challenge is to wait until the chances of success are good, and then say: "This is hard work, but I think that you can do it." The teacher chooses the right moment to put his trust on the line with students. Of course, an important part of challenge is relevance. If the required learning is relevant to the student's world of experience and has some personal meaning to him, then he is likely to work hard—*if* he feels free to try. This brings us to the question of freedom.

Freedom It is difficult for self-esteem to grow in an environment where there is little or no freedom of choice. If the student is to grow and develop as an adequate human being, he needs the opportunity to make meaningful decisions for himself. This also means that he must have the freedom to make mistakes, and even to laugh at his inadequacies. Carlton and Moore (1966, 1968) have shown that the freedom of self-directed dramatization improved the reading ability and enhanced the self concept of elementary-school youngsters. This general emphasis on freedom has been highlighted by Moustakas, who wrote: "Self values are in jeopardy in any climate where freedom and choice are denied, in a situation where the individual rejects his own senses and substitutes for his own perceptions the standards and expectations of others" (1966, pp. 4f). When the student has a say in his own development and is given personal decisions to make, he develops faith in his own judgments and thoughts.

Closely related to the notion of freedom of choice is the idea of freedom from threat. Children seem to learn and develop best in an atmosphere characterized by much challenge and little threat. Kowitz has noted, for example, that if the child feels evaluation takes place with "vicious assault upon his self concept" (1967, p. 163), there can be little real freedom. In fact, some students fear failure so much that they avoid achievement whenever they can and, when they cannot, do not try to succeed. In this way, they can avoid the task of trying to achieve. A comprehensive study of the person who fears failure is provided by Birney, Burdick, and Teevan (1969).

What this means to the teacher is that students will learn, provided the material appears to be relevant to their lives and provided they have the freedom to explore and to discover its meaning for themselves. We know that exploration is curtailed in an atmosphere in which one must spend most of his time avoiding or reducing the experience of anxiety brought about by threat to the self. Sarason (1961) has reported that a poor performance by anxious subjects occurred only when the task was presented as a threat. When anxious subjects were told that failure was normal and expected, they actually outperformed subjects who were less anxious. The freedom to try without a tiger springing at you if you fail is essential to a healthy atmosphere in the classroom.

In considering the factors of freedom and challenge, the classroom teacher can ask himself:

> *Do I encourage students to try something new and to join in new activities?*
>
> *Do I allow students to have a voice in planning, and do I permit them to help make the rules they follow?*
>
> *Do I permit students to challenge my opinions?*
>
> *Do I teach in as exciting and interesting a manner as possible?*
>
> *Do I distinguish between students' classroom mistakes and their personal failure?*
>
> *Do I avoid unfair and ruthless competition in the classroom?*

Questions like these can help the teacher evaluate himself and the classroom climate he creates.

Respect A basic feeling by the teacher for the worth and dignity of students is vital in building self concepts in them. No aspect of education is more important than the feeling on the part of the teacher that the individual student is important, valuable, and can learn in school. Sometimes teachers forget the importance of respect and run roughshod over the personal feelings of students. Using both the official and unofficial school practices which we cataloged in Chapter 3, teachers sometimes lower the feelings of worth of many young people. One of my students told me why he could never get along with his previous English teacher. It was because, although his name is Cribbidge, "She always called me cabbage whenever she called roll, and then laughed." The rule seems to be that whenever we treat a student with respect, we add to his self-respect, and whenever we embarrass or humiliate him, we are likely to build disrespect in him both for himself and for others.

If the teacher genuinely values and respects students, it will be reflected in everything he does. Davidson and Lang (1960) found that when students feel that teachers value and respect them, they are likely to value and respect themselves. Moustakas summed it up this way: "By cherishing and holding the child in absolute esteem, the teacher is establishing an environmental climate that facilitates growth and becoming" (1966, p. 13).

The need for respect is particularly important in working with culturally disadvantaged students. These are the children whose behavior makes them most difficult to respect, but who probably need respect the most. Teachers must make an extra effort to communicate to these young people a feeling of trust, positive regard, and respect. Closely related to respect is the concept of warmth.

Warmth There is considerable evidence to support the assumption that a psychologically safe and supportive learning situation encourages students to grow academically as well as in feelings of personal worth. Cogan (1958) reported that students with warm, considerate teachers produced unusual amounts of original poetry and art. Christensen (1960) found the warmth of teachers significantly related to their students' vocabulary and achievement in arithmetic. Reed (1962) concluded that teachers characterized as considerate, understanding, and friendly, and with a tolerance for some release of emotional feeling by students, had a favorable influence on their students' interest in science.

Relating more directly to the task of building favorable self concepts, Spaulding's research (1964) supported the findings of previous investigators regarding positive attitudes toward the self. He found significant correlations between the height of the self concept and the degree to which the teachers in his study were calm, accepting, supportive, and facilitative. It is interesting to note that significant negative correlations with the height of pupils' self concepts were found when teachers were dominating, threatening, and sarcastic.

An important part of warmth is commitment. Teaching has been described as a delicate relationship, almost like a marriage, where, in a sense, the teacher and student belong to each other. The student says "There is *my* teacher" and the teacher says "These are *my* students." The process of commitment is illustrated by the story of the chicken and pig who were walking down a country lane: The chicken excitedly told the portly pig of his latest business idea. "We'll prepare and franchise the best tasting ham 'n eggs money can buy, and we'll make a fortune." The pig thought it over for a moment and replied: "It's easy for you to get enthused. For you it's an occupation, but for *me* it means *total* commitment!" Perhaps total commitment is asking too much of teachers, but certainly they need to feel that their work with students is more than an occupation. A warm and supportive educational atmosphere is one in which each student is made to feel that he belongs in school and that teachers care about what happens to him. It is one in which praise is used in preference to punishment, courtesy in preference to sarcasm, and consultation in preference to dictation.

Some practical questions about respect and warmth which the teacher might ask himself are:

> *Do I learn the name of each student as soon as possible, and do I use that name often?*
>
> *Do I share my feelings with my students?*
>
> *Do I practice courtesy with my students?*
>
> *Do I arrange some time when I can talk quietly alone with each student?*
>
> *Do I spread my attention around and include each student, keeping special watch for the student who may need extra attention?*
>
> *Do I notice and comment favorably on the things that are important to students?*
>
> *Do I show students who return after being absent that I am happy to have them back in class, and that they were missed?*

It is in ways such as these that we tell the student that he is important to us.

Control Coopersmith (1967) has suggested that children who are brought up in a permissive environment tend to develop less self-esteem than those reared in a firmer and more demanding atmosphere. The assumption that clearly established and relatively firm guidance produces more self-esteem in children can also be applied to the classroom. It is important for the teacher to maintain discipline, for the type of control under which a child lives has considerable effect on his self-image. It is yet another way of telling the student that the teacher cares about him and what he does. Classroom control does not require ridicule and embarrassment. The secret seems to be in the leadership qualities of the teacher. When he is prepared for class, keeps on top of the work and avoids the appearance of confusion, explains why some things must be done, and strives for consistency, politeness, and firmness, then classroom control is likely to be maintained.

When punishment is unavoidable (and often it *can* be avoided), then it is best to withdraw the student's privileges. Of course, this means that teachers must be sure that there *are* some privileges in school which can be withdrawn. Poor control procedures would include punishing the entire class for the transgressions of a few, using corporal punishment, or using school work as punishment.

In considering classroom control, teachers might ask themselves:

> *Do I remember to see small disciplinary problems as understandable, and not as personal insults?*
>
> *Do I avoid having "favorites" and "victims"?*
>
> *Do I have, and do my students have, a clear idea of what is and what is not acceptable in my class?*
>
> *Within my limits, is there room for students to be active and natural?*
>
> *Do I make sure that I am adequately prepared for class each day?*
>
> *Do I usually make it through the day without punishing students?*

Questions such as these help the teacher to estimate his ability to handle students in a way which maintains discipline and, at the same time, builds positive and realistic self concepts in students.

Some teachers believe that warmth and firmness are in opposition to each other, but this is not so. Warmth is more than the obvious display of affection, it is also expressed by firmness which says to the student, "You are important to me and I care about the ways in which you behave."

Success Perhaps the single most important step that teachers can take in the classroom is to provide an educational atmosphere of success rather than failure. Reviewing over a dozen experiments, Wylie (1961) made the tentative statement that students are likely to change their self-evaluations after experimentally induced success or failure. This statement has been echoed in more recent studies. Costello (1964) found that over-all, regardless of the task or the ability of the students, praise produces more improvement in performance than blame. Ludwig and Maehr (1967) showed that the approval of significant others caused an increase in self-ratings and an increased preference for activities connected with the criterion task, and that disapproval resulted in a lowered self-rating and a decreased preference for related activities. Moreover, the reaction to the evaluation was followed by a spread of effect, from the areas directly approved by the significant others to related areas of self-regard.

A number of writers have pointed out some of the steps involved in giving honest experiences of success. Page's (1958) research showed that pupils' performance improved significantly when teachers wrote encouraging comments on their written work. A control group, given conventional grades without comment, lost ground. Walsh (1956) explains that it is helpful to show students that they have mastered even the smallest step, rather than vaguely saying "That's nice" about everything.

The sensitive teacher points out areas of accomplishment, rather than focusing on mistakes. Continuing awareness of failure results in lowered expectations, not learning. According to Combs and Snygg (1959) a positive view is learned from the ways people treat the learner. People learn that they are able, not from failure but from success. Questions about success which the teacher might ask himself when he thinks about success experiences for students include:

> Do I permit my students some opportunity to make mistakes without penalty?
>
> Do I make generally positive comments on written work?
>
> Do I give extra support and encouragement to slower students?
>
> Do I recognize the successes of students in terms of what they did earlier?
>
> Do I take special opportunities to praise students for their successes?
>
> Do I manufacture honest experiences of success for my students?
>
> Do I set tasks which are, and which appear to the student to be, within his abilities?

What all of this discussion hopes to say to teachers is that a backlog of challenge, freedom, respect, warmth, control, and success develops positive self-images in students and encourages academic achievement. The absence of these factors makes for the person who is crippled psychologically.

THE SENSITIVITY THE TEACHER DEVELOPS

> You can know me truly only if I let you, only if I want you to know me. . . . If you want me to reveal myself, just demonstrate your good will—your will to employ your powers for my good, and not for my destruction.
>
> Sidney Jourard, *The Transparent Self*

"Sensitivity" is a term which is used to serve many purposes and to describe various processes. In this book it is defined as the ability to sense what an individual feels about himself and the world. Sensitivity first requires the honest *desire* to become aware of how others are experiencing things. This sounds simple, but the fact is that many people don't take the necessary time and trouble to be sensitive to others. After the desire must come the habit of really listening, and listening for meanings rather than words. For instance, a student might say that he does not wish to try, when he means that it is better not to try than to try and be proved wrong.

Entering a person's private world in order to understand how he is seeing things is difficult, for the individual self can only be approached through the perceptions of some other person, perceptions filled with all sorts of prejudices, aspirations, and anxieties. Fortunately, however, most teachers have a great supply of sensitivity, as do most humans. It's just a matter of applying this sensitivity more deliberately to teaching. To the degree to which a teacher is able to predict how his students are viewing themselves, their subject, and the world, to that degree he is in a position to become a successful teacher.

Throughout this book the idea has been stressed over and over that the teacher must give the self concepts of students far greater emphasis than is presently given. The purpose of this section is to assist teachers to become more competent in assessing the self concepts of the students with whom they work. For a long time, many of us in education and psychology have been saying that theory about the self has a vital role to play in the educative process and that teachers should be made more aware of the importance of how students view themselves. Yet little has been done to equip teachers and counselors with simple clinical techniques and instruments which would enable them to be more sensitive to their students. It would seem that we in education have the responsibility, within the limits of our training, to investigate, to understand, and to utilize the self concept as a means of faciliting scholastic success. What a person says about himself, and the inferences we draw from his behavior, are valuable data for teachers. However, these are problems in understanding how students view themselves, as we shall see.

Problems in Evaluating the Self

> "First of all," he said, "if you can learn a simple trick, Scout, you'll get along a lot better with all kinds of folks. You never really understand a person until you consider things from his point of view—"
> "Sir?"
> "—until you climb into his skin and walk around in it."
> Harper Lee, *To Kill a Mockingbird*

No one, of course, can ever climb into another's skin, or see this construct we call the self, but we can infer that self in a number of ways. Two of these ways are: (1) "self-report," that which can be inferred from an individual's statements about himself; and (2) "observations," that which can be inferred from the individual's behavior. Before we turn to these methods, however, it is wise to remind ourselves that the self is multidimensional and tremendously complex and that there are two major cautions that we need to be aware of in assessing it: our *limitations* and our *biases*.

Limitations. Ideally, when you desire to assess the self, you need training and supervised experience in measurement, clinical psychology, and personality theory. Even without this preparation, however, it is possible to understand the concept of the self and to be aware of the means of measuring it. Regardless of your training, you should seek out counselors, school psychologists, and other qualified helpers to assist you in your assessments. It would also be helpful to seek out and read some of the References at the end of this book to give you a clearer understanding of the complexity of measuring the self.

Above all, keep in mind your own limitations. This means

being aware of the extent of your training and of the possible cost of errors in judgment, being able to tolerate ambiguity, not being too hasty with answers but instead trying to base your inferences on sufficient evidence, and that remembering that the self is many times more difficult to assess than is some tangible object.

Biases. It is helpful to keep in mind that a self must be studied through the perceptions of someone. Even when you try to describe your *own* self, it can only be a rough approximation. As we shall see later, one's observation of oneself is open to distortion, either involuntarily or deliberately. Therefore, in making inferences about the self, it is vital to recognize your own biases and try to take them into account as much as possible. Your task is to gain a clearer understanding of the student's self, not to try to give him yours. To put it another way, you should have a fair understanding of yourself before you attempt to evaluate the self of others.

Evaluating the self through self-reports Through the years there has been controversy over the validity and reliability of self-report inventories. One is dealing with validity when he asks the question: *Is the instrument measuring what it claims to measure?* If so, it is a "valid" instrument. One is dealing with reliability when he asks: *How consistent are the findings through various administrations?* If the findings are consistent through repeated administrations, the instrument is considered "reliable."

Rogers (1951) has taken the position that self-reports are valuable sources of information about the individual. And Allport (1955, 1961) has written that the individual has the right to be believed when he reports his feelings about himself. Both these authorities believe that if we want to know more about a person, we should ask him directly. Sarbin and Rosenberg (1955) concluded from their research that their self-report instrument was useful in getting at meaningful self-attributes quickly and with a minimum of effort. Perhaps this general viewpoint can best be summarized by a statement of Strong and Feder: "[E]very evaluative statement that a person makes concerning himself can be considered a sample of his self concept, from which inferences may then be made about the various properties of that self concept" (1961, p. 170). Numerous other studies have been based on the assumption that evaluative statements made by the individual about himself are valid and reliable data.

The major critics of self-reporting believe that while the self concept is what an individual believes about himself, the self-report is only what he is willing and able to disclose to someone else. Combs, Courson, and Soper (1963) argue that these are rarely, if ever, identical. They refer to Combs and Soper (1957), who reported that the degree to which the self-report can be relied upon as an accurate indication of the self concept depends upon such factors as: (1) the clarity of the subject's awareness; (2) his command of adequate symbols for expression; (3) social expectancy; (4) the cooperation of the subject; and (5) his freedom from threat.

Three additional variables which might influence self-reports are the familiarity of the item, response set, and social desirability. Purinton (1965) reported that changes in self-reports with repeated usage could be related to the student's familiarity with the items and would not necessarily reflect a change in his self concept. Shulman (1968) found that there are yea-sayers and nay-sayers who respond in a particular pattern irrespective of the inventory questions. Heilbrun (1965) has maintained that the social desirability of a response has something to do with its probability of endorsement on a self-report test.

Wylie (1961) concluded from her comprehensive review of research on self concept:

> We would like to assume that a subject's self-report responses are determined by his phenomenal field. However, we know that it would be naive to take this for granted, since it is obvious that such responses may also be influenced by the: (a) subject's intent to select what he wishes to reveal to the examiner, (b) subject's intent to say that he has attitudes or perceptions which he doesn't have, (c) subject's response habits, particularly those involving introspection and the use of language, and (d) host of situational and methodological factors which may not only induce variations of (a), (b), and (c) but may exert other more superficial influences on the responses obtained (1961, p. 24).

Clearly, there are a host of contaminating variables in self-reports. For the teacher, this means that conclusions about self concept based solely on self-reports must be taken with a great deal of salt. However, in spite of their weaknesses and limitations, self-reports do reveal characteristics of the self and are important to teachers. Used sensitively in conjunction with other evidence, self-reports give rich insights into how the child sees himself and his world. A few of the better known self-report inventories are listed below. For a more complete description of these and other self-report inventories, the reader is referred to Purkey (1968).

The Self-esteem Inventory. The SEI was developed by Stanley Coopersmith of the University of California. It was especially constructed for the research reported in *The Antecedents of Self-esteem* (Coopersmith, 1967). All the statements in the scale have been worded for use with children 8 to 10.

The Bledsoe Self Concept Scale. The BSCS, which was designed by Joseph Bledsoe of the University of Georgia, has been used with success from the third through the eighth grades, (Bledsoe, 1967). It consists of a checklist of 30 trait-descriptive adjectives.

The Self-appraisal Scale. Another recent self-report inventory is the SAS, developed by Helen Davidson and Judith Greenberg of the City College of the City University of New York for their research on scholastic achievers from a deprived background (Davidson and Greenberg, 1967.) It consists of 24 items, each of which has been tested for its intelligibility to fifth-grade children.

The How-I-See-Myself-Scale. This popular instrument was developed by Ira Gordon of the University of Florida from 1958 to 1967. It was devised from the categories developed by Jersild (1952), out of the compositions of children. The scale consists of a 40 (elementary form) or 42-item (secondary form) five-point scale. Additional information may be found in Gordon (1966, 1968) and Yeatts (1967).

Q-Sort. Q-sort is not so much an instrument as it is a method. It requires the subject to sort a number of self-reference statements (usually 70 to 150 items) into a series of piles or classes along a continuum of appropriateness of self-description, from those "most like" him to those "least like" him. The number of items sorted into each pile is specified in such a way that the resulting frequency distributions approximates that of a normal distribution. For an extensive reference on this method, see Cummins (1963).

Semantic Differential. The semantic differential technique of measuring the "meaning systems" of individuals was developed by

Charles Osgood of the University of Illinois. The method is described in detail in Osgood, Suci, and Tannenbaum (1957). Basically, it involves sets of polar adjectives such as Happy–sad, Hard–soft, and Slow–fast, with five to seven spaces between each set. The concept to be measured is placed at the top of the scale and the subject is to place a check somewhere along the continuum to indicate his attitude. It is a popular and flexible method of measuring the dimensions of one's system of meanings about himself and the world in which he lives.

There are other commercially produced self-report inventories which are designated to be used by individuals with special training in psychometrics. Two of the more popular are the *Tennessee Self Concept Scale* (Fitts, 1964) published by Counselor Recordings and Tests, Box 6184, Acklen Station, Nashville, Tennessee, 37212, and the *California Psychological Inventory* (Gough, 1956) published by Consulting Psychologists Press, Inc., 577 College Ave., Palo Alto, California.

Whether the self-report inventory you use is commercially prepared or locally produced, it is a good idea to remember four rules in giving self-report scales:

1. When working with younger students, items should be read to the students while the children read silently.
2. Stress the fact that there are no *right* or *wrong* answers. The student is to express those ideas he holds true about himself.
3. All self-report inventories should be administered under conditions which are as unthreatening as possible.
4. Maintain the confidentiality of the results.

Evaluating the self through observations Traditionally, observers of human behavior have been encouraged to be as passive, uninvolved, and detached as possible, in order to facilitate their learning and avoid disrupting the person being observed. The goal was to strive for objective perception of the individual and his behavior and to separate the observer's self from that which is being observed (Carbonara, 1961). In fact, the more like a camera, the more depersonalized and detached the observer became, the better.

A more recent approach to observation is that of Combs (1965a) who believes that observations are unnecessarily frustrating because "of a mistaken belief that observations must be made objectively (1965a, p. 64). He believes that sensitivity is a matter of commitment, and that the observer should be looking for *reasons* for behavior rather than at behavior itself. He explains (p. 66):

> I have given up asking my students to make coldly factual, detailed observation reports. I now ask them to do what I do myself when I watch a child behaving or a teacher teaching—to get the "feel" of what's going on, to see if they can get inside the skin of the person being observed, to understand how things look from his point of view. I ask them, "What do you think he is trying to do?" "How do you suppose he feels?" "How would you have to feel to behave like that?" "How does he see the other kids?" "What does he feel about the subject?" and so on.

It seems that Combs' approach encourages the teacher's exploration, involvement, and sensitivity to the individual.

For our purposes, we can utilize both approaches. We can be as objective as possible when making observations, and then we can be free to form our more subjective inferences.

Making observations. We can never view ourselves or anyone else with complete objectivity, for the meanings we assign things, people, and events are products of our past experience and the processes of how we view ourselves, as we have seen. Yet teachers need to minimize bias as much as possible. A good way to do this is to understand the process of observation.

In observing a person we usually begin with his appearance. We can become aware of the clothes he wears and the way he wears them. We can consider his height and weight, his posture, his grooming, and his general cleanliness. We can take note of any physical problems and his apparent state of health. Next we can take into account his behavior—his speech, his movements, his facial expressions, his manner, his habits, and his reactions. We can be particularly alert to fleeting clues which tell us how he relates to his peer group and to adults, taking into account the things he seeks out and the things he avoids, the way he reacts to success and to failure, to approval and disapproval, and the ways he spends his spare time. From all these observations we gather the raw material which we may use to draw inferences. Always, we should keep in mind that *his per-ceptions* of his appearance and behavior are more important to our understanding of him than his appearance and behavior in themselves. Sometimes a student with a seriously negative self concept will look fine.

Often it is possible for us to structure our observations by having the student respond to stimuli like those presented in structured interviews or simple quasi-projective techniques. In the structured interview, questions are carefully organized and may be open-ended. They usually deal with the student's hopes, fears, likes, dislikes, family, and school life, and are posed in an atmosphere of acceptance and permissiveness. Sacks (1966) gives a number of tips on the techniques involved in using such struc-tured interviews.

Simple quasi-projective techniques, which we can think of as the process of drawing inferences from the student's produc-tions, involve having the student evaluate himself by writing an autobiography, complete interest records, participate in play situations, or make up stories or complete sentences. The younger child's drawings can be used as indications of his self (Harris, 1963). Dinkmeyer (1965) provides some useful tips on the in-ferential aspect of child study.

Before you draw inferences about a student, it will be helpful to ask yourself: "How do I feel about this person?" "What things might distort my perceptions of how this student sees himself and others?" Try to include a number of observations on different days, to avoid misunderstandings based on a person's "off-day." Finally, avoid jumping to conclusions. If a student spends some time alone, it may stem merely from his enjoyment of solitary activities. For a more detailed treatment of methods of observa-tion, Gordon's book (1966) provides a comprehensive treatment.

Drawing inferences. Inference is a valuable scientific tool whose reliability between and within observers has been demon-strated (Courson, 1965). Once appearance and behavior have been carefully observed, we are prepared to draw some infer-ences. On the basis of what we've seen, we should ask ourselves: What are some of the beliefs he holds about himself?" "Does he see himself as a student, a leader, an athlete, a popular fellow, a son, or whatever, and in what order?" "Are his beliefs about himself generally positive or negative?" "Which beliefs are more central?" "Which are more value-laden?" "Which beliefs are most likely to resist change?" "What problems does the student have, and what is his most pressing problem *right now?*" It is in the answers we give to questions like these that we find what the individual student is like, how he feels about himself and the world, and why he behaves as he does.

One particular caution should be noted in drawing inferences, and that is the importance of being *conservative* about the use of case histories, cumulative folders, anecdotal reports, information picked up in the teachers' lounge, or any other secondary or indirect information. They involve the perceptions of a third party. While they are sometimes useful, they are also an important source of bias and misunderstanding.

In this final chapter we have seen the importance of what the teacher believes about himself and about his students, and how attitudes toward students are more important than techniques and materials. We've considered some of the things the teacher does: the attitudes he conveys, the atmosphere he creates, and the sensitivity he develops through self-report inventories and observations.

CONCLUSION

It is hoped that this little book has given the teacher an overview of theory about the self and some of the characteristics of the self; that it has explained the dynamic interaction between the self concept and scholastic success, that it has reviewed the early beginnings of the theory of the self, and that it has illuminated the task of the teacher in building positive and realistic self concepts in students.

Now it is up to you, the teacher. If the self concept is made an integral part of the curriculum it will be because you have made it happen. And the beautiful compensation of developing favorable self concepts in students is that the teacher cannot build positive self concepts in students without building his own.

REFERENCES

Abramson, P., ed. 1968. Discipline: Not the worst problem . . but bad. *Grade Teacher* 86: 151–63, 217–18.

Allport, G. W. 1937. *Personality: A psychological interpretation.* New York: Holt, Rinehart & Winston, Inc.

———. 1943. The ego in contemporary psychology. *Psychol. Rev.* 50: 451–68.

———. 1955. *Becoming.* New Haven, Conn.: Yale University Press.

———. 1966. *Pattern and growth in personality.* New York: Holt, Rinehart & Winston, Inc.

Ames, L. B. 1952. The sense of self in nursery-school children as manifested by their verbal behavior. *J. Genet. Psychol.* 81: 193–232.

Anglund, J. 1964. *Childhood is a time of innocence.* New York: Harcourt, Brace & World, Inc.

Aronson, E., and Mills, J. 1959. The effects of severity of initiation on liking for a group. *J. Abn. and Soc. Psychol.* 59: 177–81.

———, and Carlsmith, J. M. 1962. Performance expectancy as a determinant of actual performance. *J. Abn. and Soc. Psychol.* 65: 178–82.

Ausubel, D. P., and Ausubel, P. 1963. Ego development among segregated Negro children. In *Education in depressed areas*, ed. H. A. Passow. New York: Bureau of Publications, Teacher's College, Columbia University.

Avila, D. L., and Purkey, W. W. 1966. Intrinsic and extrinsic motivation: A regrettable distinction. *Psychol. in the Schools.* 3: 206–8.

Babladelis, G., and Adams, S. 1967. *The shaping of personality.* Englewood Cliffs, N.J.: Prentice-Hall, Inc.

Balester, R. J. 1956. The self concept and juvenile delinquency. Ph.D. dissertation. Vanderbilt University.

Baller, W. R., and Charles, D. C. 1968. *The psychology of human growth and development.* 2nd ed. New York: Holt, Rinehart & Winston, Inc.

Barrett, H. 1957. An intensive study of 32 gifted children. *Personnel and Guid. J.* 36: 192–94.

Bass, A. R., and Fiedler, F. E. 1961. Interpersonal perception scores and their components as predictors of personal adjustment. *J. Abn. and Soc. Psychol.* 62: 442–45.

Baum, M., et al. October, 1968. Unified effort of a junior high school faculty (NDEA Pilot Guidance Program) to "encourage success" for seventh-graders. *Reporting Res.* (Oregon Board of Education).

Benjamins, J. 1950. Changes in performance in relation to influences upon self-conceptualization. *J. Abn. Psych.* 45: 473–80.

Berger, E. M. 1953. The relation between expressed acceptance of self and expressed acceptance of others. *J. Abn. and Soc. Psychol.* 47: 778–82.

Bertocci, P. A. 1945. The psychological self, the ego and personality. *Psychol. Rev.* 52: 91–99.

Bieri, J. and Trieschman, A. 1956. Learning as a function of perceived similarity to self. *J. Personality* 25: 213–23.

Bills, R. E.; Vance, E. L.; and McLean, O. S. 1951. An index of adjustment and values. *J. Conslt. Psychol.* 15: 257–61.

———. 1959. Nondirective play therapy with retarded readers. *J. Conslt. Psychol.* 14: 140–49.

Birney, R. C.; Burdick, H.; and Teevan, R. C. 1969. *Fear of failure.* Princeton, N.J.: D. Van Nostrand Co., Inc.

Bledsoe, J. 1967. Self-concept of children and their intelligence, achievement, interests, and anxiety. *Child. Educ.* 43: 436–38.

Block, D. A. 1952. The delinquent integration. *Psychiatry.* 15: 297–303.

Borislow, B. 1962. Self-evaluation and academic achievement. *J. Counsl. Psychol.* 9: 246–54.

Brandt, R. U. 1958. The accuracy of self-estimates: A measure of self concept reality. *Genet. Psychol. Monog.* 58: 55–59.

Brehm, J. W. July, 1965. Dissonance theory as an aid in dealing with social problems. N.I.M.H. Research Project Summaries No. 2. U.S. Dept. of Health, Education and Welfare.

Brookover, W. B. 1959. A social-psychological conception of classroom learning. *School and Society.* 87: 84–87.

———. February 1969. Self-concept and achievement. Paper presented at American Educational Research Association Convention, Los Angeles.

———; Patterson, A.; and Thomas, S. 1962. *Self-concept of ability and school achievement.* U.S. Office of Education, Cooperative Research Project No. 845. East Lansing: Office of Research and Publications, Michigan State University.

————. 1964. Self-concept of ability and school achievement. *Sociol. of Educ.* 37: 271–78.

Brookover, W. B., et al. 1965. *Self-concept of ability and school achievement. II: Improving academic achievement through students' self-concept enhancement.* U.S. Office of Education, Cooperative Research Project No. 1636. East Lansing: Office of Research and Publications, Michigan State University.

Brookover, W. B.; Erickson, E. L.; and Joiner, L. M. 1967. *Self-concept of ability and school achievement. III: Relationship of self-concept to achievement in high school.* U.S. Office of Education, Cooperative Research Project No. 2831. East Lansing: Office of Research and Publications, Michigan State University.

Bruck, M., and Bodwin, R. F. 1962. The relationship between self-concept and the presence and absence of scholastic underachievement. *J. Clin. Psychol.* 18: 181–82.

Brunkan, R. J., and Sheni, F. 1966. Personality characteristics of ineffective, effective and efficient readers. *Personnel and Guid. J.* 44: 837–44.

Burns, Robert. To a louse. In *Burns: a study of the poems and songs,* ed. T. Crawford. 1960. Stanford, Calif.: Stanford University Press. p. 155.

Campbell, P. B. 1965. Self-concept and academic achievement in middle grade public school children. Ph.D. dissertation; Wayne State University.

————. 1967. School and self concept. *Educat. Leadership* 24: 510–15.

Caplin, M. D. 1966. The relationship between self concept and academic achievement and between level of aspiration and academic achievement. *Dissertation Abstracts.* 27, 979–A.

Carbonara, N. T. 1961. *Techniques for observing normal child behavior.* Pittsburgh: University of Pittsburgh Press.

Carlton, L., and Moore, R. H. 1966. The effects of self-directive dramatization on reading achievement and self concept of culturally disadvantaged children. *Reading Teacher.* 20: 125–30.

————. 1968. *Reading, self-directive dramatization and self concept.* Columbus, Ohio: Charles E. Merrill Books, Inc.

Carroll, Lewis. *Alice adventures in wonderland.* 1969. New York: The Modern Library, Random House, Inc.

Carter, T. P. 1968. The negative self concept of Mexican-American students. *School and Society.* 96: 217–19.

Centi, P. 1965. Self-perception of students and motivation. *Catholic Educ. Rev.* 63: 307–19.

Christensen, C. M. 1960. Relationships between pupil achievement, pupil affect-need, teacher warmth, and teacher permissiveness. *J. Educ. Psychol.* 51: 169–74.

Clarke, W. E. 1960. The relationship between college academic performance and expectancies. Ph.D. dissertation, Michigan State University.

Cogan, M. 1958. The behavior of teachers and the productive behavior of their pupils. *J. Exptl. Educ.* 27: 89–124.

Combs, A. W. 1962a. The self in chaos. A review of Wylie, R. C., *The self concept: A critical survey of pertinent research literature. Contemporary Psychol.* 7: 53–54.

———, ed. 1962b. *Perceiving, behaving, becoming.* Yearbook of the Association for Supervision and Curriculum Development. Washington, D.C.: Education Association.

———. 1965a. *The professional education of teachers: A perceptual view of teacher preparation.* Boston: Allyn & Bacon, Inc.

———. April 1965b. Some basic concepts in perceptual psychology. Paper read at American Personnel and Guidance Association Convention, Minneapolis.

———. Courson, C. C.; and Soper, D. W. 1963a The measurement of self-concept and self-report. *Educ. and Psychol. Measmt.* 23: 493–500.

Combs, A.W., and Soper, D. W. 1957. The self, its derivate terms, and research. *J. Individual Psychol.* 13: 135–45.

———. 1963b. The perceptual organization of effective counselors. *J. Counsl. Phychol.* 10: 222–26.

———. 1963c. *The relationship of child perceptions to achievement and behavior in the early school years.* U.S. Office of Education. Cooperative Research Project No. 814. Washington, D.C.: Department of Health, Education, and Welfare.

Combs, A. W., and Snygg, D. 1959. *Individual behavior.* 2nd ed. New York: Harper & Row, Publishers.

Combs, A. W., et al. 1969. *Florida studies in the helping professions.* University of Florida Social Science Monograph No. 37.

Combs, C. F. 1963. A study of the relationship between certain perceptions of self and scholastic underachievement in academically capable high-school boys. *Dissertation Abstr.* 24: 620.

Cooley, C. H. 1902. *Human nature and the social order*. New York: Charles Scribner's Sons.

Coopersmith, S. 1967. *The antecedents of self-esteem*. San Francisco.: W. H. Freeman and Co., Publishers.

———. February 1969. Self-concept research: Implications for education. Address presented at American Educational Research Association Convention, Los Angeles.

Costello, C. G. 1964. Ego involvement, success and failure: A review of the literature. *Experiments in motivation*, ed. H. J. Eysenck, pp. 161–208. New York: The Macmillan Company.

Courson, C. C. 1965. The use of inference as a research tool. *Educ. and Psychol. Measmt*. 25: 1029–38.

Crawford, T. (ed.) 1960. *Burns: A Study of the poems and songs*. Stanford: Stanford University Press.

Crovetto, A. M.; Fischer, L.L.; and Boudreaux, J. L. 1967. *The pre-school child and his self-image*. Division of Instruction and Division of Pupil Personnel, New Orleans Public Schools.

Cummins, R. E. 1963. Some applications of "Q" Methodology to teaching and educational research. *J. Educ. Res*. 57: 94–98.

Davidson, H. H., and Greenberg, J. W. 1967. *School achievers from a deprived background*. U.S.O.E. Project No. 2805, Contract No. OE-5-10-132. New York: The City College of the City University of New York.

Davidson, H. H., and Lang, G. 1960. Children's perceptions of their teachers' feelings toward them related to self-perception, school achievement, and behavior. *J. Exptl. Educ*. 29: 107–18.

Descartes, R. (1644) *Principles of philosophy: A discourse on method*. New York: E. P. Dutton & Co., Inc., 1912.

Deutsch, M. 1963. The disadvantaged child and the learning process. In *Education in depressed areas*, ed. A. H. Passow, 163–79. New York: Bureau of Publications, Teachers College, Columbia University.

Diggory, J. C. 1966. *Self-evaluation: Concepts and studies*. New York: John Wiley & Sons, Inc.

Diller, L. 1954. Conscious and unconscious self-attitudes after success and failure. *J. Personality* 23: 1–12.

Dinkmeyer, D. C. 1965. *Child development: The emerging self*. Englewood Cliffs, N.J.: Prentice-Hall, Inc.

Dittes, J. E. 1959. Effects of changes in self-esteem upon impulsiveness and deliberation in making judgments. *J. Abn. and Soc. Psychol*. 58: 348–56.

Durr, W. K., and Schmatz, R. R., 1964. Personality differences between high-achieving and low-achieving gifted children. *Reading Teacher.* 17: 251–54.

Dyson, E. 1967. A study of ability grouping and the self-concept. *J Educ. Res.* 60: 403–5.

Endleman, R. 1967. *Personality and social life: Text and readings.* New York: Random House, Inc.

Engel, M. 1959. The stability of the self-concept in adolescence. *J. Abn. and Soc. Psychol.* 58: 211–15.

Fair, J. 1959. A comprehensive high school studies learning. *Educ. Leadership.* 16: 351–54.

— Farber, B. 1962. Marital integration as a factor in parent-child relations. *Child Developmt.* 33: 1–14.

Farls, R. J. 1967. High and low achievement of intellectually average intermediate grade students related to the self concept and social approval. *Dissertation Abstr.* 28: 1205.

Farquhar, W. W. 1968. A comprehensive study of the motivational factors underlying achievement of eleventh-grade high-school students. U.S. Office of Education, Cooperative Research Report No. 846. East Lansing: Office of Research and Publications, Michigan State University.

Festinger, L. 1962. *A Theory of cognitive dissonance.* New York: Harper & Row, Publishers.

———. 1967. Cognitive dissonance. *Scientific Amer.* 207: 93–107.

Fey, W. F. 1954. Acceptance of self and others, and its relation to therapy readiness. *J. Clin. Psychol.* 10: 266–69.

Fiedler, F. E. 1950. The concept of an ideal therapeutic relationship. *J. Consult. Psychol.* 14: 239–45.

• Fink, M. B. 1962. Self-concept as it relates to academic achievement. *Calif. J. Educatl. Res.* 13: 57–62.

Fitts, W. 1964. *Tennessee self concept scale.* Nashville: Counselor Recordings and Tests.

Frankel, E. 1964. Effects of a program of advanced summer study on the self-perceptions of academically talented high school students. *Exceptional Children.* 30: 245–49.

Freud, A. 1946. *The ego and the mechanisms of defense.* New York: International Universities Press, Inc.

Freud, S. (1900). *The interpretation of dreams.* In *The standard edition of the complete psychological works of Sigmund Freud,* V, pp. 339–627. London: The Hogarth Press and the Institute of Psychoanalysis, 1962.

———— (1911.) The handling of dream interpretation in psychoanalysis. *Ibid.*, XII, pp. 89–96.

———— (1923.)· *The ego and the id. Ibid.*, XIX, pp. 3–63.

————. 1933. *New introductory lectures on psychoanalysis.* New York: W. W. Norton & Company, Inc.

———— 1938. *An outline of psychoanalysis.* New York: W. W. Norton & Company, Inc., 1949.

Fromm, E. 1941. *Escape from freedom.* New York: Holt, Rinehart & Winston, Inc.

———— 1947. *Man for himself.* New York: Holt, Rinehart, & Winston, Inc.

———— 1956. *The art of loving.* New York: Harper & Row Publishers.

Frost, Robert. 1916. Birches. In *Complete poems of Robert Frost.* New York: Holt, Rinehart & Winston, Inc.

Gabbler, R., and Gibby, R. 1967. The self-concept of Negro and white children. *J. Appl. Psychol.* 23: 144–48.

Gale, R. F. 1969. *Developmental behavior: A humanistic approach.* New York: The Macmillan Company.

Gibby, R. G., Sr., and Gibby, R. G., Jr. 1967. The effects of stress resulting from academic failure. *J. Clin. Psychol.* 23: 35–37.

Gill, M. P. February 1969. Pattern of achievement as related to the perceived self. Paper read at the annual meeting of the American Educational Research Association Convention, Los Angeles.

Goldberg, M. L. 1960. Studies in underachievement among the academically talented. In *Freeing capacity to learn*, ed. A. Frazier pp. 40–45. Fourth ASCD Research Institute. Washington, D.C.: Association for Supervision and Curriculum Development; National Education Association.

Goldfarb, W. 1947. Variations in adolescent adjustment of institutionally reared children. *Amer. J. Orthopsychiatry.* 17: 449–57.

Goldstein, K. 1939. *The organism.* New York: American Book Company.

————. 1963. *Human nature in the light of psychopathology.* New York: Schocken Paperbacks.

Gordon, I. J. 1966. *Studying the child in the school.* New York: John Wiley & Sons, Inc.

———— 1968. *A test manual for the How-I-See-Myself-Scale.* Florida Educational Research and Development Council. Gainesville: University of Florida.

Gough, J. C. 1956. *California psychological inventory.* Palo Alto, Calif.: Consulting Psychologist Press.

● Gowan, J. C. 1960. Factors of achievement in high school and college. *J. Counslg. Psychol.* 7: 91–95.

Haan, R. F. 1963. *Accelerated learning programs.* New York: The Center for Applied Research in Education, Inc.

Haarer, D. L. 1964. A comparative study of self concept of ability between institutionalized delinquent boys and nondelinquent boys enrolled in public schools. *Dissertation Abstr.* 25: 6410.

Haas, H. I., and Maehr, M. L. 1965. Two experiments on the concept of self and the reaction of others. *J. Personality and Soc. Psychol.* 1: 100–5.

Hamachek, D. E., ed. 1965. *The self in growth, teaching and learning.* Englewood Cliffs, N.J.: Prentice-Hall, Inc.

Harding, K. L. 1966. A comparative study of Caucasian male high-school students who stay in school and those who drop out. Ph.D. dissertation, Michigan State University.

Harris, D. B. 1963. *Children's drawings as measures of intellectual maturity.* New York: Harcourt, Brace & World, Inc.

Hawk, T. L. 1967. Self-concepts of the socially disadvantaged. *The Elementary School J.* 67: 196–206.

Heider, F. 1958. *The psychology of interpersonal relations.* New York: John Wiley & Sons, Inc.

Heilbrun, A. B., Jr. 1965. The social desirability variable: Implications for test reliability and validity. *Educ. and Psychol. Measmt.* 25: 745–56.

Helper, M. M. 1958. Parental evaluations of children and children's self-evaluations. *J. Abn. and Soc. Psychol.* 56: 190–94.

Hilgard, E. R. 1949. Human motives and the concept of the self. *Amer. Psychol.* 4: 374–82.

Holland, J. L. 1959. The prediction of college grades from the California Psychological Inventory and the Scholastic Aptitude Test. *J. Educatl. Psychol.* 50: 135–42.

Horney, K. 1939. *New ways in psychoanalysis.* New York: W. W. Norton & Company, Inc.

Irwin, F. S. 1967. Sentence completion responses and scholastic success or failure. *J. Counslg. Psychol.* 14: 269–71.

Jackson, P. W. 1968. *Life in classrooms.* New York: Holt, Rinehart & Winston, Inc.

James, W. 1890. *Principles of psychology.* 2 vols. Magnolia, Mass.: Peter Smith.

Jersild, A. T. 1952. *In search of self.* New York: Bureau of Publications, Teachers College, Columbia University.

————. 1960. *Child psychology.* Englewood Cliffs, N.J.: Prentice-Hall, Inc.

————. 1965. Voice of the self. *NEA J.* 54: 23–25.

Jourard, S. M. 1963. *Personal adjustment: An approach through the study of healthy personality.* 2nd ed. New York: The Macmillan Company.

————. 1964. *The transparent self: Self-disclosure and well-being.* Princeton, N.J.: D. Van Nostrand Co., Inc.

Keefer, K. E. 1966. Self-predictions of academic achievement by college students. *Dissertation Abstr.* 26: 4337.

Kelley, E. C. 1962a. *In defense of youth.* Englewood Cliffs, N.J.: Prentice-Hall, Inc.

————. 1962b. The fully functioning self. In *Perceiving, behaving, becoming: A new focus,* pp. 9–20. A. W. Combs (ed.) Washington, D.C.: Association for Supervision and Curriculum Development.

Kerensky, V. M. 1967. Reported self concept in relation to academic achievement in an inner-city setting. *Dissertation Abstr.* 27: 2325.

Kowitz, G. T. 1967. Test anxiety and self concept. *Childhd. Educ.* 44: 162–65.

Lamy, M. W. 1965. Relationship of self-perceptions of early primary children to achievement in reading. In *Human development: Readings in research,* ed. I. J. Gordon. Chicago: Scott, Foresman & Company.

Laury, G. V., and Murloo, A. M. 1967. Subtle types of mental cruelty to children. *Child and Family.* 6: 28–34.

Lecky, P. 1945. *Self-consistency: A theory of personality.* New York: Island Press.

Lee, Harper. 1960. *To kill a mockingbird.* Philadelphia: J.B. Lippincott, Co., p. 36.

Lewin, K. 1935. *A Dynamic theory of personality.* New York: McGraw-Hill Book Company.

Lipsitt, L. P. 1958. A self-concept scale for children and its relationship to the children's form of the manifest anxiety scale. *Child Developmt.* 29: 463–72.

Lowe, C. M. 1961. The self-concept: Fact or artifact? *Psychol. Bull.* 58: 325–36.

Lowry, H. F. 29 March 1961. The mouse and Henry Carson. Opening address, Conference on outstanding students in liberal arts colleges, Buck Hill Falls, Pennsylvania.

Ludwig, D. J., and Maehr, M. L. 1967. Changes in self-concept and stated behavioral preferences. *Child Developmt.* 38: 453–67.

Luft, J. 1966. On nonverbal interaction. *J. Psychol.* 63: 261–68.

McIntosh, D. K. 1967. Correlates of self-concept in gifted students. *Dissertation Abstr.* 27: 2403.

McNeil, E. B. 1967. *The quiet furies: Man and disorder.* Englewood Cliffs, N.J.: Prentice-Hall, Inc.

Manis, M. 1958. Personal adjustment, assumed similarity to parents, and inferred parental evaluations of the self. *J. Consltg. Psychol.* 22: 481–85.

Mann, T. *Joseph in Egypt.* New York: Alfred A. Knopf, Inc., 1938.

Maslow, A. H. 1954. *Motivation and personality.* New York: Harper & Row, Publishers.

――――. 1956. Personality problems and personality growth. In *The self: Explorations in personal growth,* ed. C. Moustakas, pp. 232–56. New York: Harper & Row, Publishers.

Maugham, W. Somerset. 1944. *The Razor's Edge.* New York: Doubleday, Doran & Co. p. 2.

May, R. 1953. *Man's search for himself.* New York, W. W. Norton & Company, Inc.

――――. 1961. The context of psychotherapy. In *Contemporary psychotherapies,* ed. M. I. Stein. New York: The Free Press.

Mead, G. H. 1934. *Mind, self and society.* Chicago: University of Chicago Press.

Meyerowitz, J. H. 1962. Self-derogations in young retardates and special class placement. *Child Developmt.* 33: 443–51.

Meyers, E. 1966. Self concept, family structure, and school achievement: A study of disadvantaged Negro boys. Ph.D. dissertation, Teachers College, Columbia University.

Morgan, E. M. 1961. A comparative study of self-perceptions of aggressive and withdrawn children. Ph.D. dissertation, University of Florida.

Morgan, H. H. 1952. A psychometric comparison of achieving and nonachieving college students of high ability. *J. Consult. Psychol.* 16: 292–98.

Morrow, W. R., and Wilson, R. C. 1961. Family relations of bright highachieving and underachieving high school boys. *Child Developmt.* 32: 501–10.

Morse, R. J. 1963. Self concept of ability, significant others and school achievement of eighth-grade students: A comparative investigation of Negro and Caucasian students. Master's thesis, Michigan State University.

Morse, W. C. 1964. Self concept in the school setting. *Childhood Educ.* 41: 195–98.

Moustakas, C. 1966. *The authentic teacher: Sensitivity and awareness in the classroom.* Cambridge, Mass.: Howard A. Doyle Publishing Company.

Munroe, R. 1955. *Schools of psychoanalytic thought.* New York: Holt, Rinehart & Winston, Inc.

Murphy, G. 1947. *Personality.* New York: Harper & Row Publishers.

Omwake, K. T. 1954. The relation between acceptance of self and acceptance of others shown by three personality inventories. *J. Consult. Psychol.* 18: 443, 446.

Osgood, C. E.; Suci, G. J.; and Tannenbaum, P. H. 1957. *The measurement of meaning.* Urbana: University of Illinois Press.

Ovid. 1955. Metamorphoses. New York: E. P. Dutton & Company, Everyman's Library Edition.

Page, E. B. 1958. Teacher comments and student performance: A seventy-four classroom experiment in school motivation. *J. Educatl. Psychol.* 49: 173–81.

Parker, J. 1966. The relationship of self-report to inferred self concept. *Educatl. and Psychol. Measmt.* 26: 691–700.

Patterson, C. H. 1959. *Counseling and psychotherapy: Theory and practice.* New York: Harper & Row, Publishers.

———. 1961. The self in recent Rogerian theory. *J. Individual Psychol.* 17: 5–11.

Peters, D. M. 1968. The self concept as a factor in over and underachievement. *Dissertation Abstr.* 29: 1792f.

Phillips, A. S. 1964. Self concepts in children. *Educatl. Res.* 6: 104–9.

Piers, E. V., and Jarris, D. B. 1964. Age and other correlates of self concept in children. *J. Educatl. Psychol.* 55: 91–95.

Purinton, D. E., 1965. The effect of item familiarity on self-concept sorts. *Dissertation Abstr.* 26: 2325.

Purkey, W. W. 1966. Measured and professed personality characteristics of gifted high-school students and an analysis of their congruence. *J. Educatl. Res.* 60: 99–104.

———. 1967. The self and academic achievement. *Florida Educatl. Res. and Developmt. Council Res. Bull.* (University of Florida) 3, No. 1.

———. 1968. The search for self: Evaluating student self concepts. *Ibid.* 4, No. 2.

Radke-Yarrow, M.; Davis, H.; and Trager, H. G. 1949. Social perceptions and attitudes of children. *Genet. Psychol. Monogr.* 40: 327–447.

Raimy, V. C. 1948. Self-reference in counseling interivews. *J. Consult. Psychol.* 12: 153–63.

Redl, F., and Wineman, D. 1952. *Children who hate.* New York: The Free Press.

Reed, H. B. 1962. Implications for science education of a teacher competence research. *Science Educ.* 46: 473–86.

Ringness, T. A. 1961. Self concept of children of low average, and high intelligence. *Amer. J. Mental Deficiency.* 65: 453–61.

Rogers, C. R. 1942. The use of electrically recorded interviews in improving psychotherapeutic techniques. *Amer. J. Orthopsychiatry* 12: 429–34.

———. 1947. Some observations on the organization of personality. *Amer. Psychol.* 2: 358–68.

———. 1951. *Client-centered therapy.* Boston: Houghton Mifflin Company.

———. 1958. The characteristics of a helping relationship. *Personnel and Guid. J.* 37: 6–16.

———. 1959a. *Counseling and psychotherapy: Theory and practice.* New York: Harper & Row, Publishers.

———. 1959b. A theory of therapy, personality, and interpersonal relationships, as developed in the client-centered framework. In *Psychology: The study of a science,* ed. S. Koch, III, pp. 184–256. New York: McGraw-Hill Book Company.

———. (1965.) The therapeutic relationship: Recent theory and research. Reprinted in *The Shaping of Personality,* ed. G. Babladelis and S. Adams. Englewood Cliffs, N.J.: Prentice-Hall, Inc., 1967.

——— 1969. *Freedom to learn.* Columbus, Ohio. Merrill Publishing Co.

———, and Dymond, R. F. 1954. *Psychotherapy and personality change.* Chicago: University of Chicago Press.

Rosenberg, M. 1965. *Society and the adolescent self image.* Princeton: N.J.: Princeton University Press, 1965.

Rosenthal, R., and Jacobson, L. 1968a. Teacher expectations for the disadvantaged. *Scientific Amer.* 218: 19–23.

———. 1968b. *Pygmalion in the classroom: Teacher expectation and pupils' intellectual development.* New York: Holt, Rinehart & Winston, Inc.

Roth, R. M. 1959. The role of self concept in achievement. *J. Exptl. Educ.* 27: 265–81.

Sacks, B. M. 1966. *The student, the interview, and the curriculum.* Boston: Houghton Mifflin Company.

Sarason, I. G. 1961. The effects of anxiety and threat on the solution of a difficult task. *J. Abn. and Soc. Psychol.* 62: 165–68.

Sarbin, T. R., and Rosenberg, B. G. 1955. Contributions to role-taking theory: IV. Method for obtaining a quantitative estimate of self. *J. Soc. Psychol.* 42: 71–81.

Schulz, Charles. 1968. *Peanuts.* New York: United Features Syndicate, Inc.

Schwarz, M. E. 1967. The effect of teacher approval on the self-concept and achievement of fourth, fifth and sixth-grade children: Case studies of seven children and seven teachers. *Dissertation Abstr.* 28: 523f.

Shaw, M. C. 1961. Definition and identification of academic under-achievers. In *Guidance for the underachiever with superior ability,* ed. L. M. Miller, pp. 15–27. Washington, D.C.: U.S. Government Printing Office.

———; Edson, K.; and Bell, H. 1960. The self-concept of bright under-achieving high-school students as revealed by an adjective check-list. *Personnel and Guid. J.* 39: 193–96.

Shaw, M. C., and Alves, G. J. 1963. The self-concept of bright academic underachievers: Continued. *Personnel and Guid. J.* 42: 401–3.

——— and Dutton, B. E. 1965. The use of the parent-attitude research inventory with the parents of bright academic under-achievers. In *The self in growth, teaching, and learning: Selected readings,* ed. D. E. Hamachek, pp. 493–500. Englewood Cliffs, N.J.: Prentice-Hall, Inc.

Shaw, M. C., and McCuen, J. T. 1960. The onset of academic under-achievement in bright children. *J. Educatl. Psychol.* 51: 103–8.

Shulman, L. S. February 1968. Multiple measurement of self-concept. Paper presented at the meeting of the American Educational Research Association, Chicago.

Sigel, I. E., and Hooper, F. H. 1968. *Logical thinking in children.* New York: Holt, Rinehart & Winston, Inc.

Snygg, D., and Combs, A. W. 1949. *Individual behavior.* Harper & Row, Publishers.

Soares, A. T., and Soares, L. M. 1969. Self-perceptions of culturally disadvantaged children. *Amer. Educatl. Res. J.* 6, No. 1.

Spaulding, R. L. 1963. Achievement, creativity, and self concept correlates of teacher-pupil transactions in elementary schools. U.S. Office of Education, Cooperative Research Report No. 1352. Urbana: University of Illinois.

————. 1964. Achievement, creativity, and self concept correlates of teacher-pupil transactions in elementary schools. In *Readings in child behavior and development*, ed. C. B. Stendler, 2nd ed., pp. 313–18. New York: Harcourt, Brace & World, Inc.

Staines, J. W. 1958. The self-picture as a factor in the classroom. *British J. Educatl. Psychol.* 28: 97–111.

Stotland, E., and Zander, A. 1958. Effects of public and private failure on self-evaluation. *J. Abn. Psychol.* 56: 223–29.

Strong, D., and Feder, D. 1961. Measurement of the self concept: A critique of the literature. *J. Counslg. Psychol.* 8: 170.

Subramuniya, Master. *Cognizantability*, one of the textbooks of the Subramuniya Yoga Order. Virginia City, Nevada: Himalayan Academy, n.d.

Sullivan, H. S. 1947. Conceptions of modern psychiatry. Washington, D.C.: William Alanson White Psychiatric Foundations.

————. 1953. *The interpersonal theory of psychiatry.* New York: W. W. Norton & Company, Inc.

Symonds, P. M. 1939. *The psychology of parent-child relationships.* New York: Appleton-Century.

Taylor, R. G. 1964. Personality traits and discrepant achievement: A review. *J. Counslg. Psychol.* 11: 76–81.

Teigland, J. J., et al. 1966. Some concomitants of underachievement at the elementary-school level. *Personnel and Guid. J.* 44: 950–55.

Tennyson, Alfred Lord. Ulysses. In *The poems and plays of Tennyson.* 1938. New York: The Modern Library, Random House, Inc.

Thomas, S. 1966. An experiment to enhance self-concept of ability and raise school achievement among low-achieving ninth-grade students. *Dissertation Abstr.* 26: 4870.

Trent, R. D. 1957. The relationship between expressed self-acceptance and expressed attitudes toward Negro and white in Negro children. *J. Genet. Psychol.* 91: 25–31.

Videback, R. 1960. Self conception and the reactions of others. *Sociometry* 23: 351–59.

Walsh, A. M. 1956. *Self concepts of bright boys with learning difficulties.* New York: Bureau of Publications, Teachers College, Columbia University.

Watson, J. B. 1925. *Behaviorism.* New York: W. W. Norton & Company, Inc.

Wattenberg, W. W., and Clifford, C. 1962. Relationship of self-concept to beginning achievement in reading. U.S. Office of Education, Cooperative Research Project No. 377. Detroit: Wayne State University.

————. 1964. Relation of self-concepts to beginning achievement in reading. *Child Developmt.* 35: 461–67.

Werblo, D., and Torrance, E. P. 1966. Experiences in historical research and changes in self-evaluations of gifted children. *Exceptional Children* 33: 137–41.

White, R. W. 1959. Motivation reconsidered: The concept of competence. *Psychol. Rev.* 68: 297–333.

Whitman, Walt. 1948. From *The complete poetry and prose of Walt Whitman as prepared for him for the death-bed edition.* Introduction by Malcom Cowley. New York: Pellegrini and Cudahy.

Williams, R. L., and Cole, S. 1968. Self-concept and school adjustment. *Personnel and Guid. J.* 46: 478–81.

Wright, B. A. 1967. *Strengthening the self-concept: Sixth annual distinguished lectures series in special education and rehabilitation.* Los Angeles: University of Southern California.

Wylie, R. C. 1961. *The self-concept: A critical survey of pertinent research literature.* Lincoln: University of Nebraska Press.

Yamomoto, K.; Thomas, E.; and Karnes, E. 1969. School-related attitudes in middle-school age students. *Amer. Educatl. Res. J.* 6: 191–206.

Yeatts, P. P. 1967. Developmental changes in the self-concept of children grades 3–12. *Florida Educatl. Res. and Developmt. Council Res. Bull.* No. 2. Gainesville: University of Florida.

Zimmerman, I. L., and Allebrand, G. N., 1965. Personality characteristics and attitudes toward achievement of good and poor readers. *J. Educatl. Res.* 59: 28–30.

INDEX